Energize Your Emotions for Life

Energize Your Emotions for Life

Practical Self-Leadership for Satisfying Relationships and Friendships

Kenneth A. Fox

WIPF & STOCK · Eugene, Oregon

ENERGIZE YOUR EMOTIONS FOR LIFE
Practical Self-Leadership for Satisfying Relationships and Friendships

Copyright © 2018 Kenneth A. Fox. All rights reserved. Except for brief quotations in critical publications or reviews, no part of this book may be reproduced in any manner without prior written permission from the publisher. Write: Permissions, Wipf and Stock Publishers, 199 W. 8th Ave., Suite 3, Eugene, OR 97401.

Wipf & Stock
An Imprint of Wipf and Stock Publishers
199 W. 8th Ave., Suite 3
Eugene, OR 97401

www.wipfandstock.com

PAPERBACK ISBN: 978-1-5326-4790-1
HARDCOVER ISBN: 978-1-5326-4791-8
EBOOK ISBN: 978-1-5326-4792-5

Manufactured in the U.S.A.　OCTOBER 25, 2018

Old Testament Scripture quotations are from New Revised Standard Version Bible, copyright © 1989 National Council of the Churches of Christ in the United States of America. Used by permission. All rights reserved worldwide.

Translations of the New Testament belong to the author.

This book would never have seen the light of day without the love, support, patience, and blessing of my wife Marilyn. To you, and to Graham, our son, this book is dedicated with love.

Let me tell you something. A man ain't a goddamn ax. Chopping, hacking, busting every goddamn minute of the day. Things get to him. Things he can't chop down because they're inside

—TONI MORRISON

All human behavior is embedded in our emotional needs, that is, in the life-long attachment system that is our uniquely human fate

—HELEN BLOCK LEWIS

Love can affect you so deeply that it reshapes you from the inside out

—BARBARA L. FREDRICKSON

Contents

Acknowledgments | ix

Preface | xi

1 Introduction: Walking a Path of Emotional Health | 1

2 How Emotions Work | 9

3 Welcome Back to the Human Race | 19

4 TLC: Take Hold of Your Emotions | 27

5 TLC: Listen to Your Emotions | 36

6 TLC: Courage to Change | 45

7 Keep Your Heart with All Vigilance | 54

8 Jesus' Sabbath: Touching Those Things That Bring You Joy | 63

9 Living inside Boundaries | 72

10 The Experience of Anger | 79

11 The Positive Management of Anger | 87

12 Shame and the Disintegration of the Self | 96

13 The Humiliated Fury of Buried Shame | 105

14 Sadness: Nights Long and Filled with Misery | 111

15 The Hideous Chamber of Horrors Called Abuse | 120

16 On the Spanking and Beating of Children | 130

17 Joy: A Satisfyingly Creative Way of Life | 139

18 Love: Where There is No Sacrifice | 148

    500 Words for Emotion | 157

    Individual or Group Study Guide | 161

    Bibliography | 185

Acknowledgments

My heart is overwhelmed with thankfulness for the family, friends, and partners who walked beside me through the researching and writing of this book. As I am fond of saying, we don't get there by going alone.

Material in this book was developed, discussed, lived, and tested at Calgary Chinese Alliance Church and Aspen Church, Calgary, where I served in pastoral roles. Thank you to my friends and colleagues for the opportunities to serve together.

In the context of teaching, pastoral care, mentoring, and seminars, I presented material in the Philippines. I taught two seminary-level courses on emotional health and leadership at Alliance Graduate School in Manila and at Ebenezer Bible College and Seminary, Zamboanga. At Asia Graduate School of Theology on the campus of Biblical Seminary of the Philippines (Valenzuela), I taught an advanced degree course on emotions in the Greek world of antiquity. I delivered weekend seminars on leadership and emotional health in General Santos at Community Evangelical Church; in Calamba at an Assemblies of God Regional Churches Conference; in Cotabato City at City Alliance Evangelical Church; and in Zamboanga at Zamboanga City Evangelical Alliance Church. *Maraming salamat* to Averell Aragon, Ben de Jesus, Roland Don S. Dulaca, Jonathan Exiomo, Lyndon Ladera, Edwin Perona, Ricky Sayco, Joseph Shao, Abigail Teh, and Joselito Toraneo, for invitations to teach.

Five people read the book in draft and provided much-valued feedback: Deborah Brooks, Rick Love, Marilyn Fox, Yan Xiang, and Angelic Que. Others engaged major portions of the book or chapters: Wing Flores, Asher Ghaffar, Jim Hardwick, Ruby Ann Kagaoan, Nharcy Laurente, Ruby Luo, Johana Mak Chan, Mary-Ellen McComb, Hansol Ryu, Toni Valderamma Dy, Hannah Toraneo, Noel Tsang, Ning Tung, and Emo Yango. They represent Canada, China, South Korea, Philippines, Taiwan, and the United States. Thank you to each of you.

Special thanks to three dear friends, Deborah Brooks, my unofficial editor and research assistant, Rick Love, for great conversations on the Hebrew Bible and emotions, and Yan Xiang, for constant encouragement and a timely suggestion that I put more of me into the book. Each of you has shown how from a generous heart flows generous actions.

I depended heavily upon several libraries for my research. I wish to thank the staffs of the Calgary Public Library, Toronto Public Library, University of Calgary Library, and Cobourg Public Library.

Preface

I WAS LOOKING FOR modest improvement in my life, enough that I could —with greater understanding and empathy—help others in my role as a leader, mentor, pastor, and teacher.

That was eleven years ago.

Lying in bed one night early in my new journey, it dawned on me that all my adult life I was exerting much self-control and self-discipline to suppress the emotions of anger, fear, and sadness. To be sure, self-control and self-discipline are excellent character qualities, worth cultivating. But I wielded them to divert my attention from issues that needed attention. Buried emotions were shaping how I felt, thought, related to people, and made decisions every day. I thought I was ruling my emotions with an iron fist; secretly, they ruled me.

Now that I am walking a path of emotional health, I have an entirely new relationship with my emotions. It is not about me ruling my emotions in an adversarial way. Rather, I think of my emotions as my best friend, a best friend who loves me incredibly much and has plenty to say to me. I explain the significance of "best friend" for walking a path of emotional health and love in the opening chapter.

As we will see in chapter 2, our emotions are as much a language of communication as words. What is more, I am persuaded that walking a path of emotional health is the most significant thing I can do if I want to nurture and promote a culture of lifelong change and growth across the tapestry of my life. My emotions are far more important than I was led to believe growing up. My emotions matter. Yours do too.

I came to see that I suffered abuse as a child, and the suppressed emotions my body hauled about were linked to that trauma. At the time, I was researching abuse and shame because much of my pastoral care focused on these areas. I decided to make myself an object of research. I thoroughly and exhaustively investigated my memories, buried emotions, and my feelings about myself. As I journeyed along this path, I wrote down my story of abuse and from time to time added details. I smile now when I think of an earlier draft, where I told my story but hid behind someone else's name. You can read my story in chapter 15.

Prior to my journey, if you had asked me how much I liked myself, I would have answered, "About a three out of ten." I used to beat myself up with thoughts of self-disgust and self-condemnation. I say "used to" because the truckload of shame, fear, disappointment, sadness, and resentment my body long carried has shrunk to the size of carry-on luggage.

Recently for fun, I learned I was born in the year of the pig according to Chinese astrology. The more I thought about it, the more appropriate it seemed. Pigs roll in the muck and have dirt-between-the-toes. That is precisely where I dwell now, tethered solidly to the ground. From childhood, I felt only disgust and shame for my body. Now, I can hardly find the right words to express the joy I own feeling entirely comfortable inside my own literal skin. I did not write it as such, but chapter 3, "Welcome Back to the Human Race," is my story. I hope it will become yours too. I have become my own best friend, and I quite like myself now, at least an eight out of ten.

Energize Your Emotions for Life is for anyone. I have a dual audience in mind. One is Christian and includes pastors. I draw stories and practical wisdom from the Bible. I occasionally talk about concerns relevant to Christians. My other audience is anyone, including leaders. This is Jesus' approach. The Sermon on the Mount is for his followers and anyone. Tenzin Gyatso, the fourteenth Dalai Lama, does the same. He is interested in helping anyone—Buddhist and not—who wants to bring change to their inner lives.

In my seminars on emotional health, I say, "Don't think attending this seminar makes you emotionally healthy." I am being funny and serious at the same time. Just as reading an exercise manual without exercising is next to useless, so is reading this book without applying the principles. This book is about change, or to borrow from Dale Carnegie, "This is an action book."

Change is sometimes easy, sometimes not, but all meaningful change takes time. We live in a quick-fix society, and this book offers no quick-fixes. *Energize Your Emotions for Life* is a self-help book. It is entirely about what we can do, and we can do plenty to bring deep transformative change to our lives.

Robert J. Sternberg says that many books like this one are "socially and scientifically irresponsible." I agree. *Energize Your Emotions for Life* is thoroughly interdisciplinary. I draw on extensive research in affective neuroscience, biblical studies, leadership, philosophy, and psychology. I also draw on cross-cultural experience, working in an Asian context in Canada and Asia. Most of the stories in the book are taken from eight years working as a pastor in two Chinese churches, twelve years teaching in the Philippines, and twenty years mentoring undergraduate and graduate students. As a biblical scholar, I have done exhaustive, critical, study of emotions across the Bible. And I have put together a practical, easy-to-understand, self-leadership book that is rock-solid in terms of foundational theory.

This does not mean, at least for me, that everything related to the human condition must be verified scientifically, but it does mean everything, including everything in the Bible, is open to questioning, doubting, testing, and analysis. I echo what Richard Boyatzis and Annie McKee say, "Good advice should be verifiable." To land on strategies of growth that work for you, there is a place for experimenting and trying different techniques. What works for one person may not work for another. But "what works" is not enough of a criterion. I would never want you to take my word for anything simply because I am convinced by what I say. In chapter 17, I talk about the importance of "challenge everything" in the context of creativity. This idea applies here.

To keep the book within manageable limits, I do not explore the connection between sexual expression and emotions. Nor do I address the role of sleep, healthy eating, weight control, and physical exercise for emotional health. Our emotions thrive in a healthy body.

I am committed to helping anyone who wants to walk a path of self-leadership and emotional health. This involves deepening a friendship with yourself, vital for getting along with others, for loving and receiving love well, and for effectively leading yourself and others to a better future. Leadership grounded in emotional health is always ethical. It extends one's integrity, character, and core values like courage, transparency, truthfulness, and love.

Walking a path of emotional health is all about love (chapter 18). My hope is that you will find this book an encouraging traveling companion for a journey to a home inside yourself where you can love and welcome love courageously.

1

Introduction

Walking a Path of Emotional Health

Alysha and Robert were dating for nearly fourteen months. Robert's good-looks made him a trophy boyfriend. He volunteered in his church's youth group and made good money upon graduating from university with a degree in oil and gas engineering. He was self-disciplined, ambitious, and courteous to Alysha's friends and parents. Alysha's mom thought he was so charming. "Alysha," her mom said, "He's one of the kindest people I've ever met." However, Robert's parents did not think Alysha was good enough for their son. They told her this and other hurtful things. Robert did nothing to protect her from their meanness. Alysha was free to meet up with her female friends but had to get Robert's permission. He always wanted to know where she was. He said it was because he cared. She felt smothered.

Robert could be delightful one minute, verbally abusive the next, and five minutes later lay a guilt trip on Alysha for not getting over it. When she tried to talk about what just happened he said she was acting like a girl, being overly sensitive, and making a big deal out of nothing. Sometimes, he would say he was sorry but make her feel she was to blame. Once he threatened to hurt her and twice he grabbed her by the shoulder. She got scared. Alysha felt she had to walk on pins and needles around him. The slightest thing could set him off. When they had a disagreement she gave in just to avoid his meltdown.

When Alyssa opened up to a girlfriend, her friend said, "God is in control and there's a reason for everything." Alysha suppressed her sadness, anger, and anxiety about their relationship by reminding herself how Robert told her God was writing their love story. She found herself believing him when he said she is the one God set aside for him. She cried a river when she opened up to Robert about how she was going through a hard time with her mom. He took advantage of her vulnerability, had sex with her even though she told him she did not want to. Afterward, he knelt down beside the couch and prayed, thanking God for their love. She knelt down in shame.

This story, thankfully, turned out well. Alysha began to attach importance to her emotions and listen to what her sadness, anger, and anxiety were trying to tell her. She deepened her friendship with herself and started to like herself. As she grew, she and Robert grew apart. With the clouds rolling away, Alysha could no longer tolerate living in a cage. She saw through his duplicity, false promises, and lies, even the nonsense about her being God's will for his life. Alysha found her voice, told Robert what she had sensed deep down for many months and severed the relationship.

Energize Your Emotions for Life is about walking a path of emotional health just like Alysha walked. It is also about practicing healthy self-leadership and becoming your own best friend, not in some self-absorbed, narcissistic way of self-worship, but as a foundation for cultivating deeper, more meaningful relationships and friendships with others.

Walking a path of emotional health is about what Jesus called cleaning "the inside of the cup," that is, our inner lives. Just how important this is can be seen in the teaching of Jesus:

> Woe to you, scholars and Pharisees, fakes, because you clean the outside of the cup and dish, but on the inside they are filled with greed and self-indulgence. Blind Pharisee, first clean the inside of the cup and then the outside of the cup will be clean also (Matthew 23:25–26).

The Greek word I translate "fakes" commonly gets rendered "hypocrites." By the time of Jesus, the word hypocrite had come to mean what we mean by it. But centuries earlier, the word was used of actors on the Greek stage. An actor wore a mask and pretended to be someone he was not. This shapes how the word is used in the New Testament and down to today. A hypocrite is someone who wears a mask, pretends, and, like Robert in the story, is one thing on the outside and something different inside. Wonderful does not come close to describing how walking a path of emotional health brings you home to yourself. You are free to take off the mask and stop pretending, you can stop acting someone else's script for you, and you can just be you.

Walking a path of emotional health is about learning to love and receive love well. When we walk this path, we are able to live the "new commandment" of Jesus, who said, "A new commandment I give to you, that you love one another. Just as I have loved you, you also should love one another" (John 13:34). As we will see in the final chapter, we can come to a place where we can open our hearts to loving others and welcoming their love.

INTRODUCTION

The Word became emotional

When we look in the Bible, we see emotions everywhere. Moses was a compassionate man who could not turn away from injustice. But he was also a resentful man prone to violence. Saul carried a lot of shame and was predisposed to be insecure, jealous, rash, violent, and narcissistic. David could be generous and humble. He could also be petty, violent, and viciously vengeful. Solomon also carried a truckload of shame and this cultivated a culture inside his heart that twisted him toward abuse of power, murder, violence, and being a sexual predator.

We see emotions all over the place when we turn to Jesus. Jesus was emotional because he was a flesh-and-blood human. The Gospel of John says, "The Word became flesh and lived among us." We have lost touch with just how dirty that word "flesh" was to first-century ears. Jesus' fleshly body was identical to ours, the same drives, functions, limitations, and neediness. Jesus was once a teenager with a teenage boy's body. If the Gospel writer wanted to use a less offensive word, other words were available. But the writer steeped as low as he could go and used that unhygienic word "flesh," because Jesus was there.

Benigno Beltran, a priest in the Philippines, lived with and served the poor for thirty years amidst, as he says, the deathly smell and continuous din of garbage trucks vomiting their load on the Smokey Mountain garbage dump in Manila. He writes of his journey in *Faith and Struggle on Smokey Mountain*. Of that place, Benigno Beltran says, "Drunken, violent fathers, negligent mothers, physical abuse, even incest added to the suffering of the young scavengers. It was very difficult not to weep while bringing abused little girls and boys to the social welfare, their faces bereft of all feeling. Their backs, arms, and legs covered with scars and bruises, proof of lives that had only known pain and despair."

Jesus did not share the same flesh as those abused little children so that he could turn around and escape to a place where he could tranquilize and anesthetize his emotions. Jesus pitched his tent on Smokey Mountain, a world filled with bruised, needy, and weary people. And he wept.

The four Gospels show us a Jesus at home with and in touch with his own emotions and constantly moved by his emotions. He was empathetic and acted compassionately. He allowed sadness and sorrow to wash over him. Jesus got angry and felt disappointments. He experienced joy and shared it with his disciples. And as we know, Jesus was overwhelmed by fear in Gethsemane almost to the point of being paralyzed. Jesus was not emotionless. You cannot when you live on Smokey Mountain.

Emotions are all over the place in our lives too. Invited or uninvited, our emotions saturate every aspect of our existence. They enter our dreams, memories, and all our relationships. They help us make sense of our past. But when we do not process our emotions well, our emotions blind us, preventing us from seeing what is important to us. There have been times when every one of us has wished we could turn off the switch and not feel.

Consequences of living emotionally unhealthy lives

Sometimes, our emotions get in the way of love. Sometimes, emotions like anger, fear, sadness, and shame damage, derail, and destroy friendships and families. In the coming chapters, I will show that the problem is not our emotions. I will suggest that, on the contrary, our emotions—or at least most of them—love us and can truly become our friend. Problems come with what we do with our emotions. We do not always return the love and friendship. When we are not in touch with our own emotions, we are unable to express our feelings in healthy ways and make relationship-enhancing, emotional connections with others. What is more, too many people live in emotional isolation, cut off from their own feelings and the feelings of others.

The consequences of living emotionally unhealthy lives are disastrous for marriages. In pre-marriage counseling I share that about forty percent of marriages in Canada and fifty percent in the United States end in divorce. I then ask, "Of those that stay together, how many are unhappy?" Answers range from a low of fifty to a high of ninety percent. Whatever the answer, when you do the math, the odds are stacked against any married couple finding fulfillment together. Were I to pick the main reason for marital dysfunction, I would put failure to take emotions seriously above in-laws, money, and sex. Failure to respect, process, and express emotions in healthy and safe ways is foundational for developing an emotionally deep and intimate connectedness and friendship with one's spouse.

Living in emotional isolation also affects the relationships of parents and children. Some parents are emotionally absent and emotionally unconnected to their children as they grow. Their children receive little nurturing, love, and emotional warmth. It does not matter what the outward reason for the emotional neglect is: off serving God, busy accumulating wealth, or just uninterested. And just as bad, lots of kids live in terror of a parent who is frightening, controlling, or emotionally out of control. When these children enter adulthood, some no longer talk to their parents. Others go through the motions of pretending to be good children. Others live in denial. Or they become just like them with their own children.

Speaking of men in particular, Calvin Sanborn says in *Becoming the Kind Father*:

> Out of touch with their inner lives, disconnected from others, many men fill their lives with addictive behavior. They become addicted to drugs or alcohol. They become addicted to their work. Or they become obsessed with television, the internet, sports, gambling, compulsive sex, acquiring things—anything to divert them from painful feelings . . . Other men numb their pain with chronic anger. Or they keep their feelings in check by obsessively controlling those around them. Many sink into the abyss of depression.

Let us not delude ourselves into thinking that addictive behavior is a male problem only. But let us stay with boys as a way to highlight problems we all face.

My favorite scene in the movie *Sleepless in Seattle* has Sam Baldwin (Tom Hanks), his son Jonah (Ross Malinger) together with Sam's friends, Greg (Victor Garber) and Suzy (Rita Wilson), chatting at Sam's kitchen table. Sam tells Greg and Suzy about how Jonah phoned a call-in radio show on Christmas Eve to say dad needs a new wife. Hundreds of women respond with letters but young Jonah is obsessed with one. Annie Reed (Meg Ryan) wrote to Sam to tell him she wants to meet him on Valentine's Day at the top of the Empire State Building. This reminds Suzy of the movie *An Affair to Remember* and she goes all weepy tears as she relates the plot. Jonah's bodily reaction to Suzy's emotion is priceless. Involuntarily, he first leans his shoulders and head back to convey distance. Then he leans forward, as though he were a doctor talking down to a patient, and asks, "Are you alright?" Greg, with a facial expression that communicates, "Jonah, women are very emotional," reassures Jonah that Suzy is fine. Sam starts mimicking Suzy's emotions, "But I cried at the end of *The Dirty Dozen*." Greg mockingly responds, "Oh, who didn't?" While Suzy continues to dry her real tears, Sam and Greg go on pretending to be all weepy tears as Sam describes how "Jim Brown was throwing these grenades down these airshafts and Richard Jaeckel and Lee Marvin were sittin' on top of this armored personnel carrier dressed up like Nazis."

All in good, mocking fun, but just about everything in our world, from fathers to schools to movies and music, tells boys like Jonah that they have to distance themselves from their emotions, and this leads to emotional dysfunction and isolation. From the cradle, boys have been taught to be emotional bricks. We boys are told never to show emotional weakness or vulnerability; rather, to keep our feelings to ourselves. We boys are taught to be decisive, independent, stable, and tough. No sissy stuff for boys is another lesson taught early. This is what we boys learned growing up in every culture around the world:

> Big boys don't cry
> Take it like a man
> Don't back down
> Don't be a chicken
> Don't be a mama's boy
> Don't be a wuss
> Don't be a sissy
> You pussy
> Suck it up

And my favorite,

> Stop crying or I'll give you something to cry about.

On a Toronto-based sports network I once heard a host describe a player, "He cried like a little girl." We boys never want to be seen crying like a little girl.

Because we boys are not taught or given permission to befriend our emotions, we are uncomfortable around emotions, whether our own or anyone else's. We learn that emotions are fluffy stuff—touchy-feely, silly, and trivial—for little girls.

Rooms in the heart

Imagine your inner life as a large house filled with lots of rooms. Your life, past and present, much of what you have experienced, felt, and thought, is inside those rooms in your heart. Each room is filled with furniture, memories of what happened. There is also air in the room, buried emotions. For just as memories get stored in rooms in our heart, so also emotions like sadness and shame, love and joy. Depending on their importance, the rooms in your heart come in different sizes, and you can move freely in and out of most rooms.

But the furniture in a few rooms may be so terrifying that you prefer to keep the lights off, the shades drawn, and the doors closed. Some rooms are lost to memory forever. Other rooms, presently inaccessible, can be recovered and entered once other rooms in your heart have had a thorough spring cleaning, so to speak. Like every metaphor, my metaphor of rooms in the heart can become clumsy and break down. For after all, when it comes down to it, our lives are one big room. To mix metaphors, everything is woven together. That is why I also like the metaphor of our lives as a tapestry, where we can bring life and light and love to every area of the tapestry of our lives.

Becoming your own best friend

With this metaphor of rooms in the heart in hand, I invite you to imagine with me that friendships can be mapped according to how much access a friend has to rooms in your heart. Pretend your life has one hundred rooms. Accordingly, your friendships may be mapped this way:

Levels of friendship	
best friend	access to all 100 rooms
close friend	access to almost all rooms
good friend	access to 50 or 60 rooms
friend	access to 30 or 40 rooms
casual friend	access to 10 or 20 rooms

As mentioned earlier, walking a path of emotional health is about becoming your own best friend. When you are your own best friend, you have walked an inner journey and come to a place where you live in and can move freely in and out of all one hundred rooms in your heart. When you are your own best friend, there are no rooms in your heart that you are presently aware of, where the lights are off, the shades drawn, and doors closed.

Most people are not best friends with themselves. Good friends yes, maybe close friends, but rarely best friends. For many people, and especially those who have experienced the trauma of abuse, there are usually a few rooms in the heart that are too terrifying to enter.

When you become your own best friend, you will find that your past will no longer blind you or trip you up. It will not paralyze you either. Nevertheless, your past is part of you, influencing your journey. But when life and light and love fill every room in your heart, you will be able to leverage your past in beautiful and life-transforming ways. As you walk a path of emotional health, you will be better prepared when tidal waves of horrible circumstances crash down on you. Like Alysha in the story above, you will find yourself liking and accepting yourself more. Comfortable in your own skin, your life will be characterized by contentment, integrity, peace, and truthfulness.

Walking a path of emotional health and becoming your own best friend is not narcissistic, selfish, or egotistical. Healthy, genuine love of self always leads to healthy life-enriching love for others. Your cup overflows. That is as true as any scientific law in the universe. When life and light and love fill every room in your heart, love gushes out.

To how emotions work we now turn.

2

How Emotions Work

Emotion and reason at war

THE SUPERSTITION THAT WOMEN are emotional and irrational—poked fun at in that scene from *Sleepless in Seattle*—has been part of human lore forever. So has the idea emotions are irrational. According to this traditional view, reason and emotion are at war and our emotions mislead us. We are told our emotions work us harm and drag us down into depravity and degradation. Emotions disturb objective and unbiased thinking. They mislead us and we are better off without them. The weapon for achieving victory in this war against our emotions is logic and reason, seen as supremely powerful to crush the enemy.

Many Bible verses appear to affirm this view that emotions are not for the godly and thus to be shunned. Psalm 46:2 says, "Therefore, we will not fear, though the earth should change, though the mountains shake in the heart of the sea" (NRSV). The reason we will not feel fear is found in verse 1, "God is our refuge and strength, a very present help in trouble" (NRSV). Connect the dots and the passage says right thinking about God removes fear from our lives. It is easy to conclude that when we feel fear, we lack faith in God. Or take Psalm 49:5, "Why should I fear in times of trouble?" (NRSV) Yes, why should a mom who depends entirely on God feel fear when her four-year-old daughter gets separated from her in a mall and is not found after three hours?

When we turn to the New Testament, Paul seems to teach that emotions like grief are inappropriate, on account of the resurrection (1 Thessalonians 4:13). Taking this passage at face value, friends of mine might then think they provoked God's disapproval when they felt sorrow when they lost their daughter to cancer. And this, despite a library of scientific research telling us we generally do not grieve long enough. Elsewhere, Paul commands believers to be anxious about nothing (Philippians 4:6). Since a command means obedience or disobedience, anxiety is interpreted as disobedience, therefore sin. In short, when we read the Bible inside the traditional view, as has been done for two millennia, we end up thinking emotions like anxiety, fear, and grief manifest lack of faith in God and sinfulness.

Given the traditional view, I ask, if anger, anxiety, fear, and sadness mislead us, cloud truth, subvert reason, and are irrational, sinful, and not trustworthy, why do we have them?

We are worse off without emotions

We have anxiety, anger, fear, and sadness as well as awe, joy, love, and thankfulness, because we need these emotions to make sense of and engage the world we live in. Most but not all emotions provide beneficial energy. And we need lots of it for moving forward with the life we want to live and for dealing with everything life throws at us.

Scientists have a clear idea what our lives would be like if we did not have emotions. We would be like patients who lack emotions due to brain injury. They can be told catastrophic news and not react. They are truly anxious about nothing; they do not shed a tear. They deny there is anything wrong; they endanger their lives. Antonio Damasio says in *Descartes' Error* that their ability to reason and plan for the future is profoundly impaired because they do not feel. The inference: lack of emotion, rather than making us smarter, makes us more irrational and can put our lives at risk.

Our emotions enable moral behavior. Put another way, our biological emotions possess at the genetic level a natural inclination to goodness. But by the unethical choices we make, we distort the genetic composition of our body's emotions, and how we express our emotions today gets twisted. With little or no empathy, guilt, mercy, and (healthy) shame, some people put others at risk. With diminished or eliminated emotions, they abuse children, lie, murder, steal, and prey on others sexually. They do it in part because they do not feel much in the way of empathy and mercy, emotions that act as inhibitors against cruelty. Unfeeling and unemotional, they are unethical, uncaring, cold-blooded, narcissistic. We were not born this way.

My wife Marilyn, our young son Graham, and I were traveling along Highway 401 in southern Ontario and we stopped for gas and a washroom break near Chatham. I was within ten feet of Graham the whole time we were inside the washroom and not for a second did I let him out of my sight. A man lurking in the washroom came and touched Graham. He hurried out immediately upon seeing me approach. Concern was in Graham's eyes. If fear is bad and gets in the way of rational thinking, did I fail by allowing Graham to feel fear in potentially harmful situations? I side with Martha Nussbaum in *Upheavals of Thought*, "A child who does not fear is a child at risk."

When we treat our emotions as the enemy and fight against them, when we try not to feel emotions, and when we suppress them, we never get rid of them. Our emotions get imprinted in our bodies, and now stored there, they are no longer our friend. They morph into a dark, heavy, toxic poison, and the storage fees we pay are astronomical in terms of our emotional, mental, and physical health. Time and again, I will come back to the matter of suppressed or buried emotions.

If all this is not enough, how would you like to be married to an emotional brick, someone not in touch with their own emotions and with whom you have little to no emotional connection?

Maybe our emotions, instead of being some irrational, bad enemy that misleads us unless we wage a war of extermination, maybe they are not so bad after all, even though sometimes our emotions feel unpleasant and overwhelming.

Reason and emotion play well together

No one disputes that our emotions can occasionally point us in the wrong direction. And nowhere is this more obvious than in "romantic love and personal relationships," where, to draw upon Daniel Goleman's *Emotional Intelligence*, "very smart people can do very dumb things."

But the opposite is just as true. Sometimes our emotions are trustworthy. Let us take Daniel Goleman's "very smart people." I have confidence that had they heeded other emotions that were calling for attention, emotions like feeling fed up, uncertain, and disappointed, then those "very smart people" may have made more prudent relationship decisions, for example, whether to stay in the relationship or manage their emotions to avoid doing dumb things. If only they had listened to those unsettling emotions that were trying to tell them something was out of joint in the relationship.

Steven Pinker says in *How the Mind Works*, "Information processing is the fundamental activity of the brain." And our emotions, an activity of the brain, are as much a language of communication as thinking. It is what the brain does. And so, when our emotions interrupt and disturb our thinking, they are not trying to make us irrational, dumb, and stupid. Not in every case, of course, but often, our emotions unsettle us so that we can think more clearly.

For sure, sometimes our emotions and reason are unreliable, a case of the blind leading the blind. How much, for example, should I trust my delicious feelings of being in-love to guide me as I decide whom to marry, if I am a mess emotionally inside? But sometimes our emotions and reason are trustworthy, even exceedingly so. The longer I walk a path of emotional health, the more I rely on what my emotions are telling me. In fact, I trust my emotions, and when my emotions disturb me, there is often good reason. After all, my emotions are trying to help me make sense of the world inside me and around me. Usually, when an emotion is triggered, it is making me immediately aware that something deserving my attention is happening or about to happen.

This brings us to one of the major claims of this book. When we walk a path of emotional health, we take our thinking and our emotions seriously. Instead of believing reason and emotion are at war, we let our reason and our emotions take each other by the hand and work together as teammates. When we do this, we are smarter and wiser for it. We will make better-informed decisions and be better equipped for navigating our way through life.

Are there negative emotions?

If my emotions love me and want to be my friend, does that mean there are no negative emotions? I have fought long and hard against labeling some emotions bad, dark, destructive, difficult, inappropriate, negative, scary, sinful, toxic, or unpleasant. For when we see our emotions by these lights, we tend to take a stance against them suitable to the label we paste on them:

- If I see fear as lack of faith in God, I try to turn the switch off;
- If I see sadness as bad, I distance myself from it;
- If I see anger as inappropriate, I run from it as fast as I can.

I believe our capacity to experience an immeasurable breadth and richness of emotion is one of life's greatest blessings. That is why I have resisted labeling any emotion by these negative labels. And I do not think anger, fear, and sadness are negative emotions just because they feel negative. We were made to be emotional. Nevertheless, as much as I want to think otherwise, some of our emotional experiences are negative.

There are the buried emotions like resentment and shame that we carry stored in our bodies. As I said above, these suppressed emotions are a destructive, vile enemy. Then there are negative emotions that should not be enjoyable but we rather enjoy them. Here are several all too common experiences: being addicted to feeling sad, taking sweet satisfaction in controlling others, getting off on a power trip of anger, and enjoying the misery of others. So yes, an emotion that feels fantastic can be negative. These emotional experiences do not love us and are not our friend. Thankfully, we can process these negative emotions in healthy ways. When we do this, good gifts come our way. Therefore, we can stand open to and welcome our negative emotions, instead of treating them as an enemy and trying to suppress them.

Emotions are beneficial energy

Most of your emotions are energy. When triggered, they disturb and move you. How powerful, then, are emotions? Erasmus satirically put emotion's power over reason at a ratio of twenty-four to one. For your pleasure, I give his words from *Praise of Folly* in full:

> So Jupiter, not wanting man's life to be wholly gloomy and grim, has bestowed far more passion than reason—you could calculate the ratio as twenty-four to one. Moreover, he confined reason to a cramped corner of the head and left all the rest of the body to the passions. Then he set up two raging tyrants in opposition to reason's solitary power: anger which holds sway in the breast and so controls the heart, the very source of life, and lust whose empire spreads far and wide, right down to the genitals. How far reason can prevail against the combined forces of these two the common life of man makes quite clear. She does the only thing she can, and shouts herself hoarse repeating formulas of virtue, while the other two bid her go hang herself, and are increasingly noisy and offensive, until at last their ruler is exhausted, gives up, and surrenders.

Daniel Goleman, Richard Boyatzis, and Annie McKee would agree with Erasmus on emotion's power. In *Primal Leadership*, they say, "Our emotions are, in a very real sense, more powerful than our intellect." I concur. Based on years of observation, I think many decisions in life are seventy percent emotion and thirty percent reason. I leave it to my readers to decide how much hyperbole is here.

Most of our emotions can be beneficial energy. Author and therapist, Beverly Engel has devoted her career to researching abuse against women and walking beside abused women on their journeys of mending. If anyone might have an ax to grind against emotions like anger, it would be she. But no. For her the problem is not our emotions. The problem is with how we process them. In *Healing Your Emotional Self*, Beverly Engel says, "As powerful and overwhelming as emotions can be, they are actually positive forces intended to help you process an experience."

Walking a path of emotional health is about learning how to process all that powerful, beneficial, emotional energy in life-enriching ways. Chapters 4–6 explain how.

How emotions work

When I was thirteen I had a crush on Julie. She hears about it from friends and meets me at my school locker. With a smile she cannot fake, she looks me in the eyes and asks if it is true. I think, do I want to blush right now? Yes. I track down the emotion of embarrassment inside my brain and trigger it. My body responds with redness in my facial color. I also decide I want to feel really embarrassed, and so I dial up that emotion to an intense nine out of ten. I also decide to add some intense heart pounding and a creaky voice, so I stimulate these bodily reactions. Then I think, wait a sec! I also want to feel in love. So I find that emotion and set it on fire. But I do not want to feel too much in-love; I have to study later. I dial down the romantic feelings to a three out of ten.

I trust you are smiling, for in real life I cannot control any of this. My facial and emotional responses happen in a fraction of a second, long before my thinking knows what is going on and can kick in. In *Emotions Revealed*, Paul Ekman reminds us what we all know is true, "Most of the time we don't have control over when we will become emotional." Our emotions are for the most part automatic reflexes and involuntary responses to stimuli, triggered without conscious deliberation on our part. Our emotions work, like most other brain functions, covertly under the scope of our awareness.

Even though our emotions operate inside our skin, they leak out. After all, everything is connected, all of one piece. One way is by involuntary bodily responses: facial expressions, fidgeting, grinding teeth, sweating, cold palms, blushing, increased heart rate, and so forth. Daniel Goleman speaks of another way in *Social Intelligence*. He says our emotions act like "neural wifi." This is especially so the more emotionally healthy we become. You sense your friend is sad without her saying a word. Your words are filled with love and concern, "Why are you sad?" With this neural wifi we create deep emotional connections and friendships with each other; sometimes we call it chemistry.

Years ago I was blessed to have a colleague who had the gift of complaining. Every time we talked, my colleague spewed slanders against the president, griped about the vice-president, whined about the dean, trashed colleagues, and ripped into students. I would be in an upbeat mood but after listening to the rants, I felt dirty in need of a shower. Whether from other people or the circumstances of life, all day long we are bombarded emotionally by what goes on around us. And our emotions are also ignited by what goes on inside us, whether physically or mentally. The other day I was walking across the campus at the University of Calgary in an airy, confident mood. A thought passed through my head and I felt dejected and heavyhearted. It all happened faster-than-instantaneous. We can no more stop these processes than we can tell a person under the shower, don't get wet.

Moods

At the office, I see it as my responsibility to show up in an upbeat mood. I want this positive mood to be entirely sincere and infectious. Moods are as contagious as colds. To do this, I practice healthy self-care, the subject matter of chapters 7–9. But when I come into the office in a grumpy mood, all I want to do is hide in my office behind a closed door.

Moods are like emotions but last longer and are usually not as intense. We all know what it is like to be in a yucky mood and to navigate around someone else's bad mood all day. Like our emotions, our moods affect how we think. When we are in a sunny mood, we have more positive thoughts. Our moods also influence how we experience emotions. When we are in a lousy mood, an emotion like anger gets triggered easier, faster, and more intensely. And our grumpy moods will act like a wet blanket and quench any pleasure we draw from positive emotions like fascination, joy, and thankfulness:

negative moods	intensify	negative emotions
negative moods	diminish	positive emotions
positive moods	intensify	positive emotions
positive moods	diminish	negative emotions

Emotional predispositions

Think of a predisposition as though it were a trigger. When the trigger is pulled, you experience certain emotions and moods easier, faster, and more intensely.

The root of a predisposition can be inherited or genetic. Scientists have long recognized that a person can have an inherited, genetic predisposition toward alcohol abuse. The same can be said for a person having a genetic predisposition toward sadness, anger, fear, or any other emotion. Having a genetic predisposition does not automatically and fatalistically predetermine one to be an alcoholic. We can never blame bad genes for bad behavior. Neither does having a predisposition toward anger cause anyone to be enslaved to anger. As Matt Ridley says in *Nature via Nurture*, "Your genes are not puppet masters pulling the strings of your behavior." Having a predisposition just means greater susceptibility and vulnerability.

Given the impulses inside me, together with my family history, I have wondered whether I have a genetic predisposition to alcohol abuse. Because of this self-awareness, I have never abused booze. Due to consistent, sound choices in this area, I look inside me now and think what Bessel A. van der Kolk says in *The Body Keeps the Score* applies to me: "Genes are not fixed." If that predisposition is still there, it is almost as harmless as a kitten.

A predisposition can also stem from our own history. An adult woman who was sexually abused as a child may react with paralyzing terror when touched—appropriately as a harmless show of affection—by a male friend. Or a man with no inherited, genetic predisposition to anger may develop an angry predisposition by having chosen to process his emotion of anger inappropriately, time after time. Eventually the response gets ingrained in our bodies. This newly-formed ingrained predisposition now exacerbates and escalates anger.

Take time to think about whether you might have a predisposition toward a certain emotion. Go through the 500 Words for Emotions chart and reflect on which emotions seem to get triggered easier, faster, more intensely, and more often. Whether genetic or due to my history I do not know, but I have always had a predisposition toward sadness. I feel it daily and occasionally I ache with sadness. I do not have a predisposition to anger but a few situations act like a predisposition to ignite my anger. I try to avoid these situations as much as possible. With a knowledge of an emotional predisposition, I warn myself when I am about to enter a situation that can trigger my anger. Just knowing is half the battle. It is also worth remembering that moderating that predisposition is going to take consistent work.

Internal emotion, its outward expression, and the gap between

What we do with anger illustrates well an essential distinction I want to make. We feel the internal emotion of anger; it is beneficial energy, and it wants to get out. But when we express our anger in inappropriate ways, this inappropriate external expression is what I call aggression. We can express aggression, for example, by beating our kids, making threatening gestures, cursing, venting, yelling, withholding expressions of love, slapping our spouse, kicking the dog, or publicly humiliating someone. Never blur this distinction between the internal emotion and its external expression. They are not the same thing. Proof: at one and the same time, we can courageously do acts of love but feel intense anger.

Let us stay with anger as our example. There is a time-gap between the experience of the internal emotion of anger and how we express that anger externally. In that time-gap in between, we decide how to respond and express the emotion. For people who have a predisposition toward anger, whether due to genetic predisposition or a history of choosing to express anger aggressively, that time-gap can be thin. But it is still there. As we will see later, there are ways to widen that time-gap so we can exercise greater responsibility and freedom in how we manage and express our emotions.

With this distinction between the internal emotion and its external expression in hand, I can return and address passages in the Bible that impress on us that we should not feel. Matthew 1:18–20 is illustrative. Mary is pregnant and not by Joseph. He plans to dispose of her. We read how an angel shows up in Joseph's dream and says, "Joseph, son of David, don't be afraid to take Mary as your wife." The angel is talking about the emotion. According to the traditional view of emotions, two paths present themselves:

1. The angel commands Joseph not to trigger the emotion of fear;
2. The angel commands Joseph to stop feeling the fear he is already experiencing.

Given the speed by which the brain processes emotions, the first is impossible. The second is maybe possible, but a huge price is to be paid for suppressing how we feel.

I offer a different way to look at this story. We can suppose the angel's command, "Don't be afraid," has to do with what Joseph does with his fear. As I read the passage, the angel appears and tells him not to let his fear get in the way of doing what needs doing. The idea is this, "Joseph, don't let your fear paralyze you from aligning yourself with God's purposes, that is, taking

Mary as your wife." It may not have been the path of honor back then, but it is the path of love. I have applied this to numerous stories in the Bible and it can work every time.

Zero tolerance for emotional stagnation

We are wired to feel anger and joy together with an immeasurable breadth and richness of other emotions. Walking a path of emotional health is not about eliminating emotions from our lives. It is about processing our internal emotions in healthy ways and making choices on how to express our emotions outwardly. We can choose aggression or take a time-out. Here is a wonderful hope wrapped in a promise: how we outwardly express our emotions, with rare exceptions, is learned behavior. Because it is learned behavior, every one of us can act responsibly and relearn how to manage and express our emotions.

To be sure, if we have a deeply ingrained bad habit or an emotional predisposition, it will take work. But there is a rope that extends all the way down to each of us. We can change. There need be zero toleration for emotional stagnation in our lives. And permit me to add, loving and accepting another person does not mean having to accept or tolerate emotional stagnation in their lives.

3

Welcome Back to the Human Race

TO EXPERIENCE MEANINGFUL, LASTING change, we look our imperfect paradise square in the face. Walking a path of emotional health and becoming our own best friend, the foundation for deeper and more fulfilling relationships with others, is never an escape from the dirt-between-the-toes. It is seeing ourselves as we are, not as we should be. Make no mistake, this can be painful, exceedingly so. But it is a path to freedom and to taking full responsibility for our lives. As we walk this path, we come to accept and like ourselves as frail, likable, normal, flawed, far-less-than-perfect human beings, profoundly deserving of love and capable of giving love. As such, we should not be surprised when we fall, slip, stumble, and experience unpleasant emotions. Nor should we be surprised when others do too.

Jesus does not beat people up

The writer of the Gospel of Matthew reached back to the Book of Isaiah to help his readers appreciate what Jesus was about. He says, "A battered reed he will not break off, and a smoldering lamp-wick he will not extinguish" (Matthew 12:20). Matthew, of course, was not talking about literal reeds along the shoreline or smoldering wicks in a lamp giving off smoke but no flame. He was talking about battered, broken, and bruised people whose light of life had all but been extinguished. They felt undervalued, half dead. Matthew said Jesus did not beat people up. Jesus did not come along and kick them in the side of the head when they were down. Jesus was, as he himself said, gentle and humble. Jesus was light and easy to bear, a place of rest for exhausted and weary people (Matthew 11:28–30).

At the time of Jesus' arrest, Peter denied Jesus three times. After breakfast some days later, sitting beside the Sea of Galilee, the resurrected Jesus restored and reassured him. Jesus told Peter, "Feed my sheep." He did not say, "Beat my sheep." That was not his way. Neither need it be ours.

The woman caught in adultery of John 8

This Jesus who did not beat people up went into the Jerusalem temple and began teaching (John 8:2–11). The religious leaders brought to him a woman they had caught in adultery. Jesus was sitting on the steps and the woman caught in adultery stood before him. The religious leaders told Jesus what the Law of Moses required; she was to be stoned to death (Leviticus 20:10). They wanted to know what he thought.

Jesus did not answer. Instead, he bent down and wrote in the dirt with his finger. Did the religious leaders think Jesus was indifferent, maybe rude to them? They kept nagging him. After a while, Jesus stood up. The story does not say this, but I can easily imagine Jesus picking up a rock and holding it out to the woman's accusers while looking each in the eye. Jesus said, "The one of you who is sinless, you get to throw the first stone." Jesus then broke his gaze, sat down, and went back to playing in the dirt.

Hearing what Jesus said, the religious leaders slipped away one by one, and Jesus was left alone with the woman. Again, he stood up. He asked her, "Woman, where are they? Is there no one to condemn you?"

"No one," the woman caught in adultery answered.

Jesus then said to her, "Neither do I condemn you. Go on your way and from now on, do not sin again."

At the beginning of this story, aside from the crowd, there were two groups of people in front of Jesus. There were the religious leaders. Being self-righteous and guardians of holiness in others, they saw the shortcomings of others easily enough. They failed to give weight to their own mess. As a consequence, they failed to see they were just like everyone else. Then there was the woman caught in adultery. She saw herself easily enough.

At the end of the story, there was only Jesus and the woman. Jesus had brought everyone down to the same place. There is no person free from moral defects who can throw stones. For in the eyes of Jesus, every one of us stands where the woman caught in adultery is. Every one of us stands beside her, whether we see it or not.

Instead of receiving judgment, condemnation, and rejection from Jesus, the woman caught in adultery received acceptance and opportunity.

This is truly wonderful: it was in her place, precisely as the woman caught in adultery, that Jesus opened for her a path for change and growth.

We can occupy the place of those religious leaders. They were blind to the state of their own hearts but quick to judge, condemn, and throw stones at anyone different from them. Or we can occupy the place of the woman caught in adultery. In the presence of Jesus, there is no other place. Are we willing, at the core of our being, to put ourselves in her place and see ourselves as the woman caught in adultery? Some people think this encourages and promotes wrongdoing, "Well, if I'm just like the woman caught in adultery, I may as well act like it." But the opposite is the case. For it is the woman caught in adultery and those beside her who receive no judgment and condemnation. From this place, the woman caught in adultery and those like her are truly free, responsible, and able to walk paths of deep transformative learning and growth, on the side of life and light and love.

The poor in spirit of Matthew 5

Jesus called his first followers and then hiked up a mountain. He sat down and taught them together with the crowds. He began, "Blessed are the poor in spirit, for the kingdom of heaven belongs to them" (Matthew 5:3). The word "spirit" can mean our inner person. Jesus is then saying we are blessed if we are poor in our inner being. We are poor in spirit when we show up empty-handed and empty-hearted, seeing ourselves as needy and bankrupt. We have nothing with which to negotiate, barter, and give so that we can get something in return. Being poor in spirit is a life-long path one walks in growing humility and teachability. It is choosing to place ourselves beside the woman caught in adultery. What we have here is a kind of humility where more and more we open our entire inner life, every room in our heart, to love life and light and love.

The sinful woman of Luke 7

Simon the Pharisee invites Jesus to eat with him at his home. During the meal an unnamed woman "who was a sinner" somehow gets into Simon's house. She brings an alabaster flask of perfumed oil and standing behind Jesus begins to cry a river. She washes Jesus' feet with her tears and dries them with her hair. If this is not scandalous enough, the woman then kisses Jesus' feet and anoints them with the perfumed oil.

The writer's purpose in Luke 7 was to show Jesus as a prophet. And so, we are not surprised to see Simon taking offense at Jesus because Jesus allowed a sinful woman to touch him. In Simon's universe, a person on the side of God will not permit her- or himself to be touched by a sinner. And if Jesus were a prophet, Simon reasons, Jesus would know supernaturally what sort of woman she was. He would prevent her from physically touching him. But Jesus was a prophet and knew who the sinners were in the room.

Jesus did not bend to the critical and judgmental expectations of people who accused him—rightly so—of being a friend to tax collectors and sinners. Jesus constantly hung out with the wrong people, loving, touching, and allowing them to touch him.

Jesus told Simon a story. Two people are in debt to a money-lender. One owes two-years' wages, the other two-months' wages. Neither of them can repay and the money-lender cancels the debts. Jesus then asked Simon, "Which of the two will love him more?" Simon replies, "Well, I guess the one who had the larger debt canceled." Jesus acknowledged this was the correct answer.

At this point Jesus turned around and looked at the sinful woman. But he spoke abrasively to Simon with his back turned to him:

> Do you see this woman? I came into your home. You did not give me water for my feet. But she washed my feet with her tears and dried my feet with her hair. You did not give me a kiss. But this woman has not stopped kissing my feet since I entered. You did not anoint my head with oil. But this woman anointed my feet with perfumed oil. Because of what she has done, I tell you, her many sins are forgiven because she loved much. But for the one who is forgiven little, well, he loves little.

Did Jesus spit out that last sentence? Jesus is the money-lender in his story. As a prophet, he has authority to forgive sins just as the money-lender had authority to cancel debts owed him. Simon is the debtor who owed two months' wages. Jesus says to him that because he has been forgiven little, he loves little. The sinful woman is the person who owed the larger debt. We learn a few verses later that she goes away in peace with her many sins forgiven. She is the person, Jesus says, who shows great love.

Simon's problem was not that he had not sinned much. It was that, like the religious leaders who brought the woman caught in adultery to Jesus, Simon did not weigh his own sinfulness. Like the religious leaders, Simon saw other people's sins. Like them, Simon—who was not poor in spirit—felt he should get what he deserves. In his mind, he had accumulated a wealth of merit in the sight of God and God owed him. And Simon felt that the sinful woman should also get what she deserves. Instead of allowing the sinful woman to touch him, Jesus the prophet should have warned her, "Woman, you cannot outrun God's judgment."

Jesus turned all this on its head. For Jesus, no matter how much the sinful woman sinned, she could not outrun love and forgiveness. It is as though love and forgiveness are in a long-distance race with sin. No matter how far sin runs, love and forgiveness outrun it. If we so choose, every time, now, forever.

As in the story of the woman caught in adultery, so here we have a choice. We can put ourselves in the place of Simon the Pharisee. Jesus says that people like him do not love much. They do not get it. They think that if love and forgiveness outrun sin, they can be selfish and abuse others. Or we can put ourselves in the place of the sinful woman of Luke 7. Of her, and people beside her, Jesus says they show great love.

The evil disciples of Matthew 7

In the Sermon on the Mount, Jesus says something that on the surface comes across as beating people up. He says to his disciples and the crowds, "So then, if you who are evil know how to give good gifts to your children, how much more will your Father in heaven give good things to those who ask him" (Matthew 7:11). Jesus calls his hearers evil, a word that could also be translated bad or wicked. Jesus says that all these evil or bad people are children of God, every last one of them. And just as these children of God know how to give good gifts to their own children, so their God and Father in heaven—"how much more"—wants to bless them with good things. By calling them evil, Jesus is not beating them up or saying they are totally depraved, not at all. Jesus is acknowledging that they are human, human just like the battered, broken, and bruised of Matthew 12, just like the woman caught in adultery of John 8, and just like the sinful woman of Luke 7.

I invite you to walk a path of inner humility and poverty of spirit and put yourself in the place of the battered, broken, and bruised of Matthew 12, of the woman caught in adultery of John 8, of the sinful woman in Luke 7, and of the evil disciples and crowds of Matthew 7. It is these people who walk paths of growth and transformation and become great lovers.

This path is not one of sacrifice (more in chapter 18), self-flagellation, and beating oneself up. Jesus does not beat us up and we do not have to either. Neither is this path one of loading ourselves with guilt and shame. Mind you, as we will see in chapters 5 and 12, there is an appropriate place for guilt and shame. I like how Larry Crabb says it in *The Safest Place on Earth*, "We are not our problems. We are not our wounds. We are not our sins. We are persons of radical worth and unrevealed beauty." We are simply walking a path to a place where we can accept ourselves as humans, immeasurably worthy and deserving of love, no different from anyone else. Welcome back to the human race.

I hope it is now crystal clear why Jesus said without qualification, "Do not judge" (Matthew 7:1). For when we are truly the battered, broken, bruised of Matthew 12, the woman caught in adultery of John 8, the sinful woman in Luke 7, and the evil disciples and crowds of Matthew 7, it is rather hypocritical to judge and condemn. In this place where Jesus invites us to live, we do not beat one another up. In love, we can speak truth into each other's lives and walk beside each other on paths of love and restoration without ever having to pick up and throw stones.

Integrity

We cannot reach flawless, blameless, unblemished perfection, and there is no use even trying. For striving for and falling short of spotless perfection only results in living lives overrun with shame, anger-turned-inward, discouragement, failure, mediocrity, and the bad kind of guilt (more in chapter 13). All this negativity, instead of encouraging us and pushing us toward excellence and love, has precisely the opposite impact. It undermines our self-confidence, it demotivates us, and it trips us up. We specialize in exaggeration, hypocrisy, and shallowness.

The integrity offered here has nothing to do perfectionism and with should, ought, or must. Rather, integrity is you just being you and projecting to others the person you truly are: no masks, no armor, no different clothes for Sunday, no phoniness, no living according to someone else's script for you. No more of what Joel Covitz describes in *Emotional Child Abuse*, "She learned, to her dismay, that she only felt loved when she wasn't being herself." People with the integrity of just being themselves have, as John C. Maxwell says in *Developing the Leader within You*, "nothing to hide and nothing to fear." Mind you, it can take a lot of courage to take the mask off and leave it off. This kind of integrity says: "*No matter what gets done and how much is left undone, I am enough.* It's going to bed at night thinking, *Yes, I am imperfect and vulnerable and sometimes afraid, but that doesn't change the truth that I am also brave and worthy of love and belonging.*" That is Brené Brown in *Daring Greatly*.

This kind of integrity, Bill George says in *True North*, frees us to integrate all aspects of our lives so we can be true to ourselves in every setting. He says, "Think of your life like a house, with a bedroom for your personal life, a study for your professional life, a family room for your family, and a living room to share with your friends." He then asks, "Can you knock down the walls between these rooms and be the same person in each of them?" Such people are not perfect, but, because this kind of integrity strengthens and energizes their courage, something necessary for living an ethical life, they are moral. For after all, this kind of integrity gives moral confidence in making the hard, ethical decisions, and especially when these decisions affect others.

Whereas the other kind of integrity that strives for perfection results in shame, anger-turned-inward, discouragement, and lots of hypocrisy, this kind of integrity lays a foundation for deep transformative change in our lives. Kind, penetrating acceptance of oneself is the basis for walking a path of life-long change, including the pursuit of excellence. Words of Carl R. Rogers, in *On Becoming a Person*, capture well what this understanding of integrity is about, "The curious paradox is that when I accept myself just as I am, then I can change."

How much can we change? (part one)

Put another way, how much better can we get? To grow old well, to have a life more and more characterized by love, joy, and peace takes steady effort. I believe that in five years, each of us can be noticeably more truthful, joy-filled, creative, generous, and thankful. If you are twenty-eight now, think how incredibly loving you can be at fifty. On the other hand, stagnant and stalled people do not grow old quite so well. As time goes by, their lives are more and more characterized by anxiety and joylessness, controlling and manipulative behavior, a grumbling and complaining attitude, and lack of appreciation and thankfulness.

Walking a path of change starts where each of us is today. If we honestly and truly want to change, we can. There are no valid excuses or rationalizations for not growing old well. As we walk a path of emotional health we become more confident, courageous, forgiving, generous, humble, joyful, loving, peaceful, and truthful. As we make healthy choices, we become less arrogant, controlling, greedy, grumbling, impatient, judgmental, quarrelsome, selfish, and vain. As we face our future, we can be encouragingly optimistic about how much we can change.

What about our past? We cannot sweep or pray away the past, but we can change our relationship to it. Our past will always be with us; it is only a matter of how we carry it into our future. I introduced the metaphor of rooms in the heart in chapter 1. I asked you to imagine your inner life as a large house filled with lots of rooms. Your memories are the furniture. Depending on the furniture, the air in the room can be buried emotions like sadness and shame, love and joy. Our brains have tremendous capacity to hold on to traumatic memories permanently.

Not always, but sometimes we can come to a place where the unpleasant memory endures, but we feel nothing or nearly nothing; where formerly, the memory triggered emotions that overwhelmed us. Thankfully, some of our traumatic memories, stored in various rooms in our heart, can be stripped of an emotional trigger. If only the emotional trigger could be removed from every traumatic memory. Who knows, maybe it can for one or two people. But—and how I wish this were not so—some residual, enduring emotion can remain attached to some traumatic memories. The arrows point both ways. When we remember a traumatic experience from our past, the memory can trigger intense emotions like sadness and shame that potentially can overthrow us. And the experience of an emotion can bring back into awareness a traumatic memory that we wish to forget. For sure, we can experience some reduction in the intensity and power of the residual, enduring emotions attached to traumatic memories. Whereas before, the emotion triggered might have been an eight or nine out of ten in intensity; now it might be a more manageable four or five.

I prefer the word mending for our inner life and not the word healing. For me, the word healing carries the idea, "as though it never happened." We see this in Jesus' healing of a man with a withered hand (Matthew 12:9–14). Jesus healed the man's hand, and as a result, the hand was exactly like the one that had not experienced trauma. For me, to apply the word healing to our inner life means, it is as though the traumatic abuse of our past never happened. This can only happen by pretending and living in denial.

We are all broken. And just like broken things, as we face, own, process, and fully integrate everything from our past onto the tapestry of our lives, we can mend to varying degrees. Some people experience significant mending in their inner lives, whereas others, less so. It has nothing to do with lack of faith, fate, God, bad luck, or bad genes.

No matter how much or how little our hearts mend, we can fully embrace and integrate our past onto the tapestry of our lives, but only when, thoroughly and exhaustively, we get to the bottom of our own story. Or to switch metaphors, we can come to a place where we can move freely in and out of every room in our heart. We can be our own ever true best friend and live fully in the present.

Thankfully, in incredibly beautiful ways, broken and mended people can leverage their entire story to bring life and light and love into the lives of other broken people.

4

TLC

Take Hold of Your Emotions

Take hold of your emotions

Listen to your emotions

Courage to change

ALICE MILLER SPENT HER childhood in Poland and Germany and survived the Second World War by disguising her Jewish heritage. She became a psychologist and turned to writing about child abuse, something she knew all too well. Her mother did not want her. She portrayed herself to Alice as the embodiment of motherly self-sacrifice but saw Alice's needs as tiresome demands to be viciously punished with slaps to the face. In *Breaking Down the Wall of Silence*, Alice Miller said, "The needs and questions of this little girl simply ricocheted off the wall."

To reduce the child to helpless subservience, her mother alternated between cold indifference and towering rage. She humiliated Alice and ignored her for days on end. She insensitively accused Alice of one thing or another. She viewed Alice's attempts to defend herself as disrespectful attacks. More ferocious punishments followed.

Her mother still expected Alice to honor and love her. Alice dared not question her mother's sadism. "To maintain the illusion of her love," she created a web of lies. She said, "To have realized the truth would have killed me." Alice tried to bury her natural need for affection and love. She told herself that if she needed nothing from her mother, if she sacrificed herself for her mother, if she denied herself, she would eventually receive the love she ached for. But all she got was isolation and loneliness. Filled with shame and self-hatred, she believed she was totally depraved.

For nearly sixty years Alice suppressed her emotions about how her mother abused her. She was intellectually aware of what happened but "didn't dare *feel* this reality." She barricaded herself from her emotional life and her own story. She said, "The price for this flight from reality turned out to be high indeed."

Eventually Alice Miller walked the heart-wrenching journey to the truth. She uncovered, articulated, and evaluated the truth of her childhood trauma. She gave herself permission to feel her childhood despair and loneliness, including the shame and rage of an abused child. She breathed life into frozen emotions. She stopped blaming the wrong person, herself, and held her mother appropriately responsible (more in chapter 15). She accepted the truth her mother did not love her.

Walking a path of emotional health is about learning to deal with the emotions we encounter today. And like Alice Miller, it is also about going deep inside, excavating all the buried emotions and memories of our past, and giving them a voice.

"There's no problem so big that I can't run from it" —Charlie Brown

The only way a child can deal with the paralyzing trauma of abuse is to run away from emotions and memories that torture and torment. This shields children from volatile anguish and keeps them breathing. But for a teen and adult, running from buried emotions and memories by suppressing or denying them fills one's inner life with more fear, resentment, sadness, and shame, provoking depression and emotional disorders.

Marie was an affectionate, fun-loving, and intensely alive kid who at fourteen lost her mom suddenly to cancer. Over the next few years she became superficial and shallow, a shell of her former effervescent self. Marie did not give herself permission to weep and feel deeply the loss of her mom who loved her completely. Marie suppressed her painful emotions and disconnected from herself. It does not help when we say, "You'll get over it." It was not in Marie's best interest to get over it. It was in her best interest to feel her aching heartbrokenness. She needed lots of time to grieve her loss. But she did not give herself permission to grieve, and, my guess is, others did not either. Taking hold of our emotions means letting the tears flow like a river.

We bury our emotions when we do not experience our emotions as they come to us. Suppressing our emotions takes these forms:

- denying, ignoring, and minimizing them;
- pushing, medicating, and praying them away;
- ruminating over them;
- inflicting them on others in aggressive, relationship-damaging ways;
- exaggerating them.

That Alice Miller achieved massive suppression of her emotions and memories for so long testifies to how powerful suppression is as a mechanism for not truthfully and lovingly facing one's past and present emotions. We exert much emotional energy to keep a lid on them. But the suppressed emotions stored inside us are energy. They find a way out and hijack the thoughts, emotions, and moods we experience today, and more so the older we get. Put differently, they are like a high-powered vacuum cleaner sucking in and poisoning today's emotions. Buried emotions are like an ill-tempered dog that growls, barks, and bites.

Buried emotions together with emotions we experience today are stone-deaf to "do not," "must not," and "should not." When we tell our emotions these things, we end up shutting our eyes and telling ourselves and others we do not feel. More frequently, we beat ourselves up with guilt and shame, because we still feel anxiety, despair, and other difficult emotions. But the most popular strategy is to bury our emotions inside ourselves. The problem is, suppressing emotions, while successful today, fails in the long run. The passing of time never mends. Time works against us when it comes to dealing with suppressed emotions. "When I'm ready, I'll deal with it" is a tactic of avoidance and makes things worse.

Feel better, pop a pill

Suppressing difficult emotions is a powerful but fundamentally unsuccessful strategy to avoid facing the inner anguish, intolerable realities, and unresolved issues from our past. So is addiction. Why bother laboring at self-leadership and walking a life-long path of emotional health when you can pop a pill? Sigmund Freud, after all, had his addictions to cocaine, cigars, and his daughter Anna to manage his overwhelming emotions and inner chaos.

Alcohol, caffeine, research, smart phones, cigarettes, cocaine, marijuana, power, abusing and controlling organizations and others, movies and television, mutilating the body, physical violence, social media, excessive physical exercise, prescription and over-the-counter drugs, sex, sugar, compulsive spending, music, video games, over-work, and God and religion, can all morph into addictive drugs. This list could go for a couple pages.

Our addictions dampen, quench, and suffocate the difficult emotions we experience. They numb the pain and help keep a lid on the torment that buried emotions and memories cause. But resorting to addictions does not address deeper issues or produce transformative growth. In *The Noonday Demon*, Andrew Solomon says, "The rebuilding of your self cannot be achieved with any drugs that now exist." Addictions do not deliver one outcome that results from walking a path of emotional health.

To be sure, we all need some, what I call in fun, emotional cocaine. There is nothing wrong with an occasional escape from reality. I come at this again in chapter 17 when I share "Work 3:1 into your daily routine." I took this idea from Barbara L. Fredrickson and apply it to how we can nurture joy in our lives. We all need to go to the beach, whether literal or figurative. Emotional cocaine, whether a beach, a hike in the mountains, a delicious book, or time with a close friend, makes us feel better. And in those times when an emotion seems too overwhelming, there is something to be said for focusing on something else, but only until we can get back on our feet and face what triggered the emotion (chapter 5).

When we get enslaved to our escapes from reality, they become addictions. No addiction is benign or harmless. For sure, our addictions keep a lid on buried memories and emotions, but, as I said in chapter 2 and will say again, the storage fees we pay are astronomical. We replace freedom with compulsiveness and imprison ourselves in a destructive darkness that has nothing to do with life and light and love. Addictions cloud and darken reality. Addictions twist, damage, and disconnect us from our natural ability to feel emotions and empathetically feel the emotions of others. Some addictions damage the body; many more damage families and friendships.

Is venting okay?

When Ke is in a stew, she barfs chunks of steaming-hot fury all over her husband and teenage daughter. She feels better afterward, and her relief reinforces doing it again. But is venting okay because she feels better after? How do husband and daughter feel? They are drenched in emotional puke.

Ke feels better but at what cost? Does venting bring about an intelligent dialogue that identifies what triggered her venting and results in problem solving? It is impossible to listen and think straight when venting. Or will Ke, once she feels relief, ignore the whole thing? Does her venting incite her husband and daughter to vent back? Have you ever yelled at someone because they yelled at you? When her daughter yells back, will Ke evaluate that behavior as inappropriate and discipline her daughter? Put another way, will Ke be intolerant of behavior in her daughter that she tolerates in herself?

What about the upsetting memories Ke's venting will plant in husband and daughter? As I said in chapter 3, our brains hold on to memories like these permanently. Will this matter to Ke? Where will she draw the line between venting anger and verbally abusive behavior? Will Ke's venting create distance between her and her family? A pot boiling over scalds everyone the boiling water touches.

Venting takes no talent, training, or effort. But self-deception blankets us when we think it is okay, even beneficial. Venting butchers relationships and is a monumentally pointless waste of time.

The better way, managing our emotions (TLC), takes training and occasionally rigorous work:

> Take hold of your emotions (this chapter)
> Listen to your emotions (chapter 5)
> Courage to change (chapter 6)

Take hold of your emotions

I had a boss who operated behind my back to undermine projects I worked on. He spread lies about me and manipulated people to oppose the projects he himself had approved. When I got wind of this from two colleagues, I felt three natural, normal, and healthy emotions: disappointment, betrayal, and anger. I knew that if I did not take these feelings seriously, they would seep down into rooms in my heart and morph into resentment and lethal hatred, fuel for gossip, bitterness, righteous indignation, and slander. They would damage my character, core values, and behavior. Doing nothing was not in my best interests. I took hold of my emotions and gave myself permission to feel them fully. As I dislike feeling angry, this was not pleasant. I thoroughly journaled my emotions and thoughts over the course of several days and feel nothing now when I remember. A satisfying outcome.

Taking hold of your emotions means becoming fully present to and aware of what you are feeling. You grab hold of your emotions with both hands—metaphorically speaking—and not let go. The key is to deal with your emotions as you experience them, in the moment or shortly after, and for as long as necessary. When tempted to suppress them, tell yourself, If I do not deal with my emotions now, I will have to later. It will be much harder then, and a residue of bitterness, resentment, or hatred may endure permanently.

As unbearable as it can be, give yourself permission to be present to your emotions, to embrace and feel them. What does this look like? Imagine two friends. You are with your friend in a restaurant, sitting across from each other, talking away, and looking into each other's eyes. You are one hundred percent fully present to your friend and your friend is one hundred percent fully present to you. Your attention is not divided between friend and cell phone. Now imagine your friend is your emotion, which of course it is.

Read at a snail's pace what Barbara L. Fredrickson says in *Love 2.0* about how you can take hold of your emotions, "Whatever the feeling, there's no need to push it aside. Pleasant or not, let the feeling in. Accept it as part of what it means to be you in this moment. Meet the feeling with curiosity and openness. Explore it. Note how this feeling registers in your body and how those bodily feelings change—subtly—from one moment to the next."

Taking hold of your emotions means putting into words how you feel. Look at the 500 Words for Emotions chart and search for the word(s) that describe how you feel. You can start by selecting one of the twenty-two broad categories: affection, agitation, anger, and so on. To bring precision, look at words in each category. Describing how you feel can sometimes be strenuous but sometimes easy. Language does not always permit precision; you are putting into words emotions that are nonverbal. Honesty can be difficult if you think it shameful or sinful to be angry, anxious, or afraid. Thankfully, your emotions are not like an unlearned foreign language. They are your love language for speaking to yourself, and they want to be understood. The more you work at it, the better you will get.

Next, without minimizing or exaggerating, describe how mild or intense your emotion is. I like to use a scale of one (mild) to ten (intense). Assign your emotion a number. Obviously, the higher the number, the more cause for concern for emotions like anger, fear, sadness, and shame.

There will usually be a bunch of emotions mixed together inside you. The more you take hold of your emotions, the better you will get at telling them apart and describing each one.

Pay attention to how your emotions express themselves throughout your body. A few years ago, I learned first-hand the value of listening to my body, which for me has always been harder than listening to my emotions. I was under a lot of stress at work. I felt it in my neck and was agitated and restless. The stress affected sleep and short-term memory. One morning I was putting on my socks. With one sock in hand, I looked around for the other. Where was it? You guessed it, on my foot. Short-term memory, muscle tension, facial expressions, heart-pounding, breathing, headaches, problems with bowels, sweating, stomach-in-knots, diminished sex drive, posture, grinding teeth, physical agitation, shaking, and sleep patterns are some involuntary changes that our emotions trigger in our bodies. This is not surprising. We are not assembled from parts. Everything is one seamless whole.

There is no downside to journaling

Consider journaling as you walk a path of emotional health. Your emotions love you, and journaling is one way for your emotions to find their voice. In *The Nice Girl Syndrome*, Beverly Engel says, "Journaling can be a powerful tool for self-discovery. Your journal can act as a silent companion that listens without judgment. It can reflect back to you aspects of yourself you have never been aware of."

This should be reason enough but there is more. Just thinking about our emotions is a waste of time. I am not exaggerating. It is next to impossible to fight against our tremendous capacity for self-deception so long as we ruminate about our emotions inside our head.

Think of your skin as a barrier. Your skin separates what you think and feel inside your body from what is going on outside you. What you need to do is grab hold of what you are thinking about your emotions, carry those thoughts across the barrier of your skin, and write them down. Once your thoughts are written down, you can see them more clearly and reduce your capacity for self-deception. With persistent probing and patient questioning, you can grind away until you see more clearly what needs seeing.

Here are six tips that help me and may work for you:

1. Approach journaling with conviction, grittiness, and resolve. Rarely will you journal if you wait until you feel like it;

2. Do not use journaling to hurry an emotion; do not treat journaling as a drug to numb or escape emotional pain;

3. Your journal needs to be private. When you write for an audience you will not be as honest as you need to be;

4. Do not feel you need to journal every day, and you do not have to journal every detail of your life. With time, you will sort out what needs attention;

5. I have found this little gimmick helpful for getting started. I tell myself I will write one paragraph. That gets me going and then take all the time necessary;

6. Write first, edit later. If I try to polish the thought inside my head, it stays there. After I get it out, I can revise it.

"Excuse me, everyone, give me a moment to process my emotions"

Suppose you are in a meeting where a colleague says something that triggers your anger. It would be inconsiderate to mentally check out of the meeting to process your emotions there on the spot. Besides, there is no need.

This is what I do when I cannot take hold of my emotions as I feel them. Laugh if you like but this works for me. I silently tell my anger, "I will deal with you." Knowing I will give my anger my full attention later helps me to calm myself, so I do not say something sarcastic in the meeting. I am managing, not suppressing, my emotions.

Can we over-analyze our emotions?

In *Terminator 3*, John Connor (Nick Stahl) and Kate Brewster (Claire Daines) are in a motor home while the Terminator (Arnold Schwarzenegger) drives. Skynet will trigger nuclear annihilation at 6:18 p.m. that day and they are fleeing the coming fallout. In the back John and Kate are warming up to each other. The Terminator looks back and says emotionlessly, "Your levity is good. It relieves tension and the fear of death." Smiles drain from their faces, the chemistry evaporates, and John goes back to making bombs.

You may know someone who kills by over-analysis. You want to scream in exasperation, "Please, give it a rest." In taking hold of our emotions, can we analyze them to death? Yes, we can, when we ruminate over and over inside our skin about how we are feeling but do not do anything about it. And there is no need to take hold of every emotion, not by a long shot. To repeat, with time we learn to sort out those emotions that deserve attention and those we can pass over.

But over-analysis is usually not the issue with respect to those emotions that deserve our attention. The problem is not looking at them thoroughly enough. Let me explain, using suppressed emotions and memories as an example.

I met Nicole for the first time when she was twenty-six years old. She grew up in the Philippines and had experienced abuse as a child and teen. She has rooms in her heart filled with memories of abuse and suppressed emotions. She opens the door to that room and puts a foot inside and feels pain. She compulsively keeps doing this over and over. I have wondered whether she is addicted to sadness. Nicole's problem is not over-analysis. It is lack of full, exhaustive analysis. She needs to enter and be fully present in that room. She needs to take all the time necessary, as excruciatingly painful as it will be, to fully see, feel, and deal with everything in there. And when she does, that part of her past—to switch metaphors—will be fully integrated onto the tapestry of her life. That room in her heart, which formerly was filled with resentment and shame can now be filled with life and light and love. Nicole can move freely across the entire tapestry of her life; she can own her whole story and expand her own inward freedom and peace.

5

TLC

Listen to Your Emotions

Take hold of your emotions
Listen to your emotions
Courage to change

As part of transformative self-leadership, we open our hearts and take our emotions by the hand. After all, our emotions love us and, if not already, want to be our friend. Once we think we have been thorough in describing how we feel (chapter 4), we can take the next step and listen to what our emotions are telling us. We ask, why do I feel the way I do? Or, what are my emotions telling me?

Sometimes the reason why we feel the way we do is obvious

I suspected the student had plagiarized in the past but could not prove it. This time I did. The policy of the seminary said course failure. To show the extent of plagiarism, I marked the student's paper and the source extensively in yellow highlighter—not a couple careless pages—and submitted both to the dean. The student successfully appealed, passed the course, graduated, and became an ordained minister.

A few years later I spoke at the church where the individual had pastored. A couple approached me and we had lunch. They told me in tears how they had trusted this pastor because the person was a seminary graduate. This minister defrauded them out of many thousands of dollars, then left to lead another church when the church board got involved. The couple's stress over the matter was so severe, one of them had been hospitalized. I said that when the person applied to the seminary, the student's pastor wrote a letter advising strongly against their admittance to the school. I also said the student plagiarized an entire paper for a course, but no penalty was levied. I felt their pain, betrayal, disillusionment, and anger. I also relived the frustration, disappointment, and anger I felt over how the dean handled the matter.

More recently, I sent my friend Yan a chapter of a novel I am writing. She cried reading it and told me I had to keep sending her more. I was rapturous when I heard her encouraging words. In both episodes, had I asked myself why I felt as I did, the reasons would have been transparent. Discovering what my emotions are telling me oftentimes takes no time and effort.

Sometimes the reason is confusing or obscure

I feel sad and ponder whether it is that predisposition to sadness I mentioned in chapter 2. My sadness is triggered easier, faster, and more intensely than any other emotion. Other times, I feel sad because I am exhausted. When I am drained, any sadness caused by circumstances in my day will be aggravated. When I am recharged (more in chapter 7), my sadness diminishes or disappears. It is usually not difficult to untangle why I feel the way I do in situations like these.

But frequently I am sad and can point to any number of causes. I hold one problem responsible, but it could easily be another. In there beside my sadness, I also see other emotions like anger, agitation, and fear. These can make answering the question, why do I feel the way I do? seem like digging through slimy mud. In addition, I said in chapter 4 that the suppressed emotions we carry around inside our bodies leak out and hijack the thoughts, emotions, and moods we experience today. It will be worth our while to look to those buried emotions for part of the reason we feel the way we do.

In short, there are occasions when it takes back-breaking excavating work, and we still may not get to the bottom of why we feel as we do. This is because—to mix metaphors—the reason we feel the way we do remains confusing or obscure, hidden behind clouds that do not clear away, no matter how much we persist. Waiting a few hours or a day can sometimes help, and we will make progress by journaling. But even then, we do not always succeed in seeing clearly. Some days the clouds do not give way to blue skies.

Our emotions: a love language

In the previous chapter, I said our emotions are a love language. I take this terrific phrase from Gary Chapman's *The 5 Love Languages*. When Joseph's brothers heard their father had died, they became distressed and afraid (Genesis 50). These emotions were a language of love, warning them to be alert. What sparked these emotions was not confusing: they had sold Joseph into slavery, and dear brother may want to return the favor. The emotions they experienced were logical and prudent. But Joseph's magnanimous kindness enveloped them, and I imagine their distress and fear vanished like potato chips on New Year's Eve. Alysha listened to the love that her anger, disappointment, and fear communicated to her (chapter 1). Though it took time, she eventually broke off the relationship with Robert. Her emotions were on her side and had things to tell her that she needed to hear. They were as much a voice of communication and reason as her thinking (chapter 2).

We befriend and transform our emotions when we pay attention to the message they have for us. When we have listened, one of two things usually happens. Since most emotions are beneficial energy, they provide energy to do what needs doing (chapter 6). Or they evaporate and disappear.

Core values, emotions, and behavior

I remember the day I resolved to pursue excellence. I was twenty-five and tired of being good, good at school, good at music, good at sports, good at everything. I was determined to pursue excellence and saw what had to be done: start saying no to some things, so I would have more time to pursue excellence in a few things. I had been doing too much. Pursuing excellence became bred in the bone; let me use Ed Catmull's words from *Creativity, Inc.* to explain what this looks like for me now, "It was unthinkable that we not do our best."

Pursuing excellence has never been difficult or a sacrifice, and it has made my life so much simpler. It made me teachable. Giving expression to this core value has helped me see where my strengths lie, what I have burning passion for, and equally important, what I have no passion for. With it, I cultivated a culture of self-discipline and self-leadership across the tapestry of my life. Pursuing excellence energizes me emotionally, and I like the person I am when I pursue excellence. A dear friend likes this in me too. She told me she lives this core value because of me. I was not surprised when she said this. I have known her long enough and well enough to know this predisposition to pursue excellence was in her heart all along.

Core values, like excellence, live inside us. They powerfully, tenaciously, and comprehensively shape behavior, decision-making, other core values, relationships, and how and why we feel the way we do. We know core values are inside us if we have knowingly nurtured specific ones. But some happen as a result of habit, and we can be oblivious to some, especially the dark ones, which I will discuss below. Any character trait can be a core value. In addition to excellence, I cultivate the core values of creativity, generosity, joy, love, teachability, truth, and thankfulness.

If you are old enough to have watched writer-director George Lucas's *Star Wars*, you know moviemaking changed forever in the summer of 1977. Two years later with lots of money in his pockets, George Lucas created a computer division and that meant a search for a computer executive. Ed Catmull, who would co-found Pixar Animation Studios and serve as President of Pixar Animation and Disney Animation, was flown to California. During the interview, they asked him, "Who else should Lucasfilm be considering for this job?" Ed Catmull furnished names without hesitating. In *Creativity, Inc.*, he explains why he offered the names of people he thought were doing impressive work:

> My willingness to do this reflected my worldview, forged in academia, that any hard problem should have many good minds simultaneously trying to solve it. Not to acknowledge that seems silly. Only later would I learn that the guys at Lucasfilm had already interviewed all the people I listed and had asked them, in turn, to make similar recommendations—and not one of them had suggested any other names!

Where Ed Catmull speaks of worldview, I speak of core values. To stay with my language, he lived the core values of humility, teachability, generosity, and we don't get there by going alone. His core values spoke into his day-to-day decision-making, habits, leadership, relationships, and how he felt.

Ed Catmull was entrusted with the stewardship of leading George Lucas's new division. But let us give wings to our imagination and pretend otherwise. Back in New York, the reject letter lands on his desk, and he decides on a brisk walk in Central Park. As he walks he remembers how he provided Lucasfilm with names of highly-qualified individuals who competed against him. He wonders if he had been foolish to name names. But this thought cannot set down roots and his core values blow it away. For underneath his disappointment that blue Monday is a soft and gentle sense of confidence for having been true to his core values. In our make-believe story, Ed Catmull's core values took each other by the hand and banded together to modulate his emotional response and reassure him that his behavior aligned with what he knew was the right thing to do.

In the diagram below, treat the arrows as lines of influence, how our behavior, core values, and emotions give shape to, transform, and protect each other:

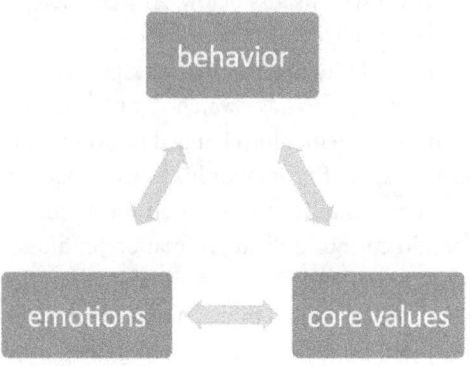

The core value of truth

Suppose you have truth as a core value. It molds you and leads your decision-making and courses of action. And because your emotions are a love language, feelings of confidence and gladness reinforce truth-guided behavior. As this core value becomes more rock-solid, the easier it becomes for you to speak and live truth, and not misrepresent it. This dynamic explains how the longer we walk a path of real change, the easier change is.

Misrepresenting the truth is not hard to map. A colleague was fired and then asked to write a resignation letter. Upon receipt of the letter, it was announced that he resigned, no mention of being terminated or having to write the letter. We misrepresent the truth when every word that comes from our mouth is true, but people listening go away thinking something other than the complete truth. Key pieces of information were withheld. Misrepresenting the truth is deceptive trickery and lying, even when our hearts do not condemn us.

If we have truth as a core value, feelings of guilt wash over us when we lie or misrepresent the truth. Our emotions and core values work together to make us suffer and feel miserable for violating what we value. I appreciate how the emotion of guilt benefits. Guilt does not want us to do something stupid again, something not true to who we are.

Emotions and fundamental needs

Our emotions together with our behavior and core values are also tethered to needs, desires, or longings deep inside us. Everything about us is, as I said, a seamless whole. I purposefully leave vague what these needs may be for each of us. I share Alice Miller's basic longing to be loved. These central needs also make up what I think of as our dark side, that aspect of us that can damage others and ourselves. As I will show below, I am bringing dualistic language to something about us that is not dualistic, unnatural, or unhuman.

However, there was a time in the not-so-distant past when I judged as selfish, shameful, and sinful my inmost desire to be loved. Since my early teenage years, I hated my basic needs. But now, I have befriended my fundamental human longings and have learned how these needs express themselves across the tapestry of my life. I see how my desire to be loved works itself out as my dark side, to use someone for my own selfish gratification. But I also see how my desire to be loved—on the side of life, light, and love—anchors me as a human and the person I want to construct. I see that when I hated this basic need to be loved, I was hating myself.

Instead of separating myself from my inmost longing to be loved, I embrace it. I have integrated it into my life, and it has rewarded me. It wages war against my pride and arrogance, and it expands my heart, so I can love and be loved from a place a self-acceptance, vulnerability, and interdependence. My inmost neediness to be loved has made me a beautiful person.

When emotions are not our friend

It comes as no surprise that I like speaking of our emotions as loving us as our friend. There is an exception. Some core values do not stand up in the daylight. Core values like arrogance, greed, obsession with power, self-absorption, and using other people for personal gratification make the human heart uninhabitable. As automatic as gravity, our emotions align with these dark core values and, consequently, stop acting as a friend.

This applies to leadership. Through the constancy of gnarled and twisted habits, some people strip their emotions of their natural moral compass and join them to dark core values. This union breeds selfish, thick-skinned, unethical, shallow, brittle, and insensitive individuals. And since leadership extends a person's character, people like this in leadership cut through people's lives like the blade of a guillotine. They long for power and will be emotionally exhilarated and energized when they get power and use power to control others and institutions. Except as a buzz phrase and doublespeak, leadership as stewardship is meaningless to them. They abuse power and cannot conceptualize that their behavior could ever be abusive.

Just as we can change how to express our emotions, so we can change our core values when they are dark or childish. We saw in chapter 4 how Alice Miller convinced herself that if she denied her own neediness and sacrificed herself for her mother, she would eventually win her mother's love. She internalized self-deception, and those dark core values were woven into the fabric of her life, giving body to her emotions and behavior. When Alice Miller's own natural and healthy neediness surfaced, she was overwhelmed by guilt, shame, and self-loathing. For she had drilled into herself that her own needs simply did not matter. I can relate.

Because these core values were so deeply ingrained into Alice Miller as a child, it took her years and years of speaking truth against the self-deception she had swallowed. After an excruciatingly long, painful journey of relearning and mending, she came to see that her own neediness did matter. She saw there was nothing shameful or wrong with needing and wanting love from a human being. I can effortlessly imagine that Alice Miller felt truckloads of guilt and shame as she spoke truth against the self-deception. Thankfully, she rewrote her core values and her emotions aligned to her new reality. But emotions are slow to learn, and that is why we need to be patient with them as they readjust to our new reality.

Our core values grow more powerful or weaken, depending on whether we reinforce or violate them. As we saw, the more we speak the truth, the stronger our core value of truth gets. It gets easier to tell the truth, and when we fall, our core value helps us get back on our feet. As the diagram above illustrated, our core values express themselves in outward behavior and emotions, and our behavior and emotions strengthen and reinforce our core values.

What is more, our core values will shine a bright light as we develop a deeper friendship with ourselves and others. Here is a beautiful, heart-transforming promise: if we nurture positive core values like forgiveness, generosity, love, thankfulness, and truth, we are going to find ourselves liking ourselves more and more. And people who share similar values are going to love us too, heart touching heart.

Our tremendous capacity for self-deception

Selena's parents were pastors in an evangelical church tradition where, if the husband was a pastor, the wife was too. Most of the time, they were off burning out for Jesus, giving it all to God (more in chapter 9). But when her pastor-father happened to be home, Selena lived in terror of his physical, emotional, and verbal violence. As her parents were not home much, Selena was passed off to extended family. These uncles, aunties, and male and female cousins sexually abused Selena too many times for her to count, all before she reached the age of eleven. Because of the trauma of emotional neglect and the physical and sexual abuse, she retains one memory prior to age six, running away from her pastor-father in her underwear, filled with terror when she was four.

Selena told me she was so filled with rage and hatred toward her parents and God. And because hatred retraces its steps and consumes the one who hates, she loathed herself in toxic shame and self-disgust. She told me, "My parents hate me, and God hates me. I'm getting what I deserve." In high school and Bible college, Selena preyed on her male and female friends for sex. She allowed herself to enter an abusive relationship with a young man who attended her parents' church and went to Bible college, training to be a pastor. It all looked so sweet on the outside, and her parents bragged about how their daughter was dating a pastor. But he was emotionally, physically, and sexually abusive toward her. The pastor-in-training raped her three times. She was also raped by her supervising pastor while on internship.

To interpose, this supports Beverly Engels' observation from *The Emotionally Abused Woman*, "Emotionally abused women are drawn to emotional abusers like moths to the flame."

Mom's birthday comes, and Selena writes her a letter in a birthday card, saying how much she loves her and how her mom is her best friend. Her mom knows nothing of what Selena endured. Selena cannot express enough thanks for her mom's warmth, unconditional love, and for always being there to support her through all her difficulties growing up. For Selena, her mom has forever been apple pie and ice cream. Selena tells mom she wants to be exactly like her. Her mom did nothing to protect Selena from her husband's physical, emotional, and verbal abuse. Her mom had little time for her growing up (emotional neglect). Her mom neglected the stewardship of this child entrusted to her care, to fill her with love, protection, and lots of companionship as she grew. Unless Selena cuts through the self-deception, embraces the truth of her past and her parents' role, and she gives herself permission to grieve the loss of love she never had, it is as likely as not that Selena will turn out exactly like her mom (more in chapter 15).

I mentioned earlier that when we lie or misrepresent the truth and have truth as a core value, guilt makes us suffer. But we will feel nothing or next to nothing when there is no core value of truth inside us. Our tremendous capacity for self-deception kicks in here. We think we have truth as a core value all evidence to the contrary: we do not feel guilty when we lie.

We have tremendous capacity for self-deception. Sometimes, as in the lives of Alice Miller and Selena, we want to shield ourselves from painful and uncomfortable emotions, memories, and realities. We create webs of illusion about ourselves and others. We also have tremendous capacity to reduce our self-deception by walking a path of emotional health, which includes growing in self-awareness.

Is truth sometimes bad for us?

In his 1884 play, *The Wild Duck*, Henrik Ibsen puts into the mouth of a character, "Yes, the saving lie [also rendered "the vital lie"]. It's what sustains life in all of us," and "You take away the life-lie from the average man, and you take away his happiness with it." There seems to be something to this. In researching this book, I was knocked off my feet by the number of psychologists who say illusion and ignorance are sometimes preferable to the truth. For them, some self-deception is bliss. They feel that for those who have experienced trauma, the best thing to do is cauterize the emotional wounds and live in ignorance. Others think medication is the ticket.

I disagree. If we cannot see clearly into our inner lives, then aspects of our inner life are dark or—to use another metaphor I like—covered with clouds. To use my language, becoming best friends with ourselves means opening our eyes wide, clearing away the clouds, and bringing life and light and love to every area of our lives or into every room in our hearts. It is what it means to become our own best friend, the foundation for deeper and more meaningful relationships with others. All our inner darkness cannot be removed; all of clouds' illusions cannot be blown away. But our illusions and ignorance can be significantly reduced.

For sure, facing the truth of our past can feel unbearable; taking hold of all those buried emotions and memories can be agonizing. But as Alice Miller says in *The Body Never Lies*, "Feelings do not kill." Our emotions are not dangerous. Problems and emotional disorders come from not facing the truth. The full truth, or as much as can be recovered, has incredible power to set us free. There is nothing like living in freedom across the entire tapestry of our lives, as our own best friend.

6

TLC

Courage to Change

Take hold of your emotions
Listen to your emotions
Courage to change

John Wayne said, "Courage is being scared to death and saddling up anyway."

A friend of mine needs to learn the truth about what happened to her when she was a child. Some large holes on the tapestry of her life need filling. This means meeting with her mother, but they have not talked in twenty years. Were she to meet her mother, she would, rather predictably, be overwhelmed by agitation and hesitancy to the point of being unnerved. Regardless of how she aches to get distracted by the clutter of living, she can push through her fears and arrange a meeting. With some luck, some of her emotions will provide her with beneficial energy to step on the bus. We regret not changing.

Courage to take hold of today's fears

We feel awesome one moment and wretched the next, all because we have one thought. If only our fears vanished as fast. Every so often, speaking truth to our fears gets rid of them. This is what I think happened to the distress and fear of Joseph's brothers when they saw that their brother had only love for them (chapter 5). But more often not so fast. No matter. We can speak truth to today's fears, so they do not get in the way of doing what needs doing. When we speak truth to our fears, they usually respond well, even if slow to get on the page. Suppose you long to say I love you to someone who means the world to you, but fear grips you. You tell yourself the truth that you would love to hear these words from her; you will not regret saying it; your heart fills these words. Speaking truth to our emotions helps you gain confidence and freedom to act courageously and say I love you.

Do not underestimate the benefits that come from embracing common daily fears. In chapter 17, I will share how I put an idea from Mihaly Csikszentmihalyi into action: I do things out of character for me. To quote from that chapter, "It takes courage to go left when I normally go right." It is the first day of class and I feel two-out-of-ten fear about introducing myself to the person sitting beside me. I push through my apprehensiveness and do it. As I take hold of my small daily fears, I mature in courage, confidence, and self-control. For, as often as not, after a hurricane comes another hurricane, and to lean into the storms, I need the strength that this growing integrity of character provides.

To regulate daily emotions like fear and anger, and calm my body, I do relaxation and deep breathing exercises for five to seven minutes, five to seven times a week. It is an enjoyable habit, and I do it even when I feel fine. I sit comfortably on a hard surface with my feet planted on the floor about a foot apart. I sit up straight with my shoulders back and hands resting on my thighs. I slowly and deeply breathe in for six seconds and then breathe out even slower. I focus on breathing. When my thoughts drift, I bring them back to my breathing.

For managing today's emotions (TLC) and walking a path of self-leadership, speaking truth to our fears, pushing through small daily fears, and doing body-calming exercises are beneficial. But their value as strategies for change is reduced unless we act on what we know we need to change. Knowing what needs to be to changed and then not doing it restricts our capacity to change in the future. Change turns out to be just noise and brings no fundamental alteration in ourselves.

Courage to take hold of buried fears

I said in chapter 2 that, according to the traditional view of emotions, "Do not fear" means striving to be free from fear: we do not let fear get rolling, or we stamp fear out as soon as it does. The former is unattainable, I said, given how fast our brains trigger emotions. And suppressing our fears comes at enormous cost. I know. I bet the farm and lost. My body hauled about—to reuse a metaphor from the Preface—a truckload of fears. I knew the buried fear was there because, for most of my life, I employed two methods against them. One tactic was to cast my fears on God in prayer. The other was to quote Bible verses at my fears. My favorite was Isaiah 41:10, "Do not fear, for I am with you, do not be afraid, for I am your God; I will strengthen you, I will help you, I will uphold you with my victorious right hand" (NRSV).

I expended much effort not to fear, but my fears did not go away. To repeat what I said in chapter 4, our emotions are deaf to "do not," "must not," and "should not." Telling my fears not to fear was not the message my fears needed to hear. All I did was bury them inside me. But suppressed emotions are energy and find a way out. My fears twisted and distorted how I thought and made decisions. I was scared to death of living the life I wanted to live, and so I lived the life others, whom I looked up to, wanted for me. I saddled up but saddled the wrong horse. Regret mauled me.

In that same chapter, I described how Alice Miller was aware of what she endured but "didn't dare *feel* this reality." I can say the same. From childhood, I knew my fears hemmed me in and triggered my predisposition to sadness. The strategies I harnessed were ineffective in reducing the paralyzing power of fear. My fears have shrunk substantially because I did what I wish I had done decades ago: I took hold of my fears (chapter 4) and did not let go until I explored—thoroughly and exhaustively—what was in those rooms in my heart where my fears lived (chapter 5). I have more fight in me today than ever before to chase my dreams.

We don't get there by going alone

To be sure, self-reliance and self-sufficiency are exemplary core values. But only to a point. To navigate 10,000 obstacles, to stop my fears from tripping me up, and to cross rivers of transformative change and career development, I have learned we don't get there by going alone. This truth has been uncomfortably torturous to move from my head to heart. I preferred to figure things out and do it myself. Being autonomous and independent is bred in my bones.

But I have always needed lots of hugs and the safe heart of a best friend to pour my heart into. I just denied I did. Today, I respect this need (more in chapter 18). I see that selfishness has two sides. The poisonous side needs no comment, but there is a selfishness on the side of life, light, and love. I would never have said that two years ago. I selfishly crave and need the courage and encouragement that the one person extends to me.

In *Conquering Fear*, Harold S. Kushner says, "Any path is easier to travel when you have somebody's hand to hold." Having a traveling companion for my journey is an invaluable gift. Without this gift, I would not, over the long haul of life, reach the level of excellence I want for my career and my personal formation. I like what Richard Boyatzis and Annie McKee say in *Resonant Leadership*, "It is a lot harder to stop the process of developing yourself when you have other people invested in helping you change." The one who loves me brings out the best in me, but I had to step outside my pride, risk vulnerability, and choose to be interdependent.

Courage to take full responsibility

I said in chapter 4 that we can treat God as an addictive drug to avoid facing painful issues in our lives. We can also use God to lift the burden of responsibility off our shoulders. Nowhere is this more readily seen than in the theology that God is a matchmaker. It goes like this: God knows exactly the type of person you need and is preparing that right person for you. God will work circumstances to bring the two of you together. Your role, wait for God's perfect timing.

We do not need the Bible to tell us just how irreconcilable this is with being individuals who can take control of and responsibility for our lives. But when we look to the Bible and the New Testament, in particular, we see something entirely different from this irresponsible lunacy. At 1 Corinthians 9:5, Paul asked, "Do we not have freedom to take along a believing wife as the other apostles do and the brothers of the Lord and Cephas?" There is only one correct answer, "Yes, Paul, you have freedom, freedom to get married if you want; freedom not to, if you don't. You're responsible and it's up to you."

At 1 Corinthians 7:8–9, Paul said, "I speak to the unmarried and widows; it is well for them to remain as I myself am; but if they cannot control themselves, let them marry." Paul did not say, "We unmarried people need to wait patiently on God. For those of us who are meant to marry, God is preparing a perfect match. We need to wait and not take things into our own hands." Rather, Paul told the unmarried it is not a bad idea to stay single. But he then adds that if they want to get married, go ahead. Unmarried people are free to marry, free not to, it is up to them. God is no matchmaker. When we turn to the Hebrew Bible, the couple places in the Book of Genesis where God acts as a matchmaker are exceptions and have to do with the creation of the people of Israel.

Using God to escape responsibility can also be seen in our "I feel God is" talk:

- I feel God is calling me to marry her
- I feel God is calling me to be a missionary
- I feel God is calling us to build a new church building
- I feel God is calling me to go to seminary
- I feel God is calling me to full-time ministry

Five pastors applied for a leadership role in a Christian organization in Canada. Four of the five said in their cover letter they felt God was calling them to the position. As we will see in chapter 15, this kind of talk slips easily into spiritual abuse. Not once in the New Testament do we see this "I feel God is" talk. Not once do we see people determining God's will by appealing to "I feel God is." Not once do we see God leading people by their emotions. God, I suppose, can do all this. All I am saying is, nothing in the New Testament says God does.

Do not get me wrong. Our emotions help us in powerful ways in sorting out our world, in seeing what needs changing in a situation or relationship, and in decision-making. As I said, it is in our best interests to listen to our emotions. But there is nothing in the New Testament about God speaking or leading through our emotions. And this extends to the feeling of peace in decision-making. The presence or absence of the emotion of peace is no indication that something is the will of God.

Mind you, some think Philippians 4:7 does. Paul said, "The peace of God, which surpasses every manner of thinking, will guard your hearts and thoughts in Christ Jesus." Let us observe what the verse says and does not say. Paul said the peace of God guards the hearts and thoughts of believers. This peace of God, however, has nothing to do with emotion. It is something quite different. What Jesus experienced in the Garden of Gethsemane the night before his crucifixion illustrates what Paul had in mind. The last thing Jesus felt was some inner, emotional peace and tranquility. Quite the opposite, he was overwhelmed by emotional turmoil, despair, uncertainty, and fear. But what Jesus had in that dark hour was conviction, a deep, inner confidence and assurance he was where he was supposed to be. This is what Paul was talking about.

Sigmund Freud said, "Most people do not really want freedom, because freedom involves responsibility, and most people are frightened of responsibility." As true as this is, I believe each of us can walk a path to a place where we are free to be fully self-responsible for everything in our lives, including our decision-making and how we express our emotions. Whether we are frightened of this or not, Oprah Winfrey is right, "You are solely responsible for your life."

Courage to express our emotions responsibly

In chapter 2, I said that between the internal emotion and its external expression is a time-gap. It is inside this time-gap where a decision is made, consciously or not, how our inward emotions will be expressed outwardly, in appropriate or inappropriate ways. The time-gap is small, so small that some people do not think it is there. And so, when they yell, they say, "I could not help myself." But we know the gap is there because the husband will throw his cell phone at his wife when no one else is present but not throw it when others are. He can control himself after all.

Of course, some external expressions of inward emotions are part of our genetic programming and cannot be changed. I could repeat Charles Darwin's experience at the London Zoo, but I have my own. When my son Graham was young, we had a Toronto Zoo membership. Every week, Graham and I would get there as soon as the zoo opened so we could see the animals wide awake before the tourists and school kids came and the animals hid or went off to sleep. One morning the snow leopard was strolling around the cage. Between us and the cage was a wooden railing, and Graham slipped under it and stood between it and the cage a meter away. Graham was safe. Seeing Graham as a tasty morning snack, the snow leopard darted with lightning speed at him. I jumped before I knew I jumped. My brain perceived danger and ignited a biologically-determined physical reaction.

Other external expressions of our inward emotions are as subconscious and as they are fast. But the difference here is, we learned these external expressions. Compare it to typing on a keyboard. I look at the computer screen and type without consciously thinking or looking at the keyboard. If I stop to think, I know the letter s is to the right of the letter a. But what is beside the s? I had to look. Through constant repetition and lots of looking, I learned the layout of the keyboard, so much so that I can type without thinking where the letters are. My brain thinks it can manage this task and thousands of others without having to engage conscious input from me.

Similarly, through conscious repetition, and often reinforced and drilled into us by cultural and parental expectations, we program into our brains how to express our emotions outwardly. As a result, the outward expression of the inward emotion can be almost as fast and automatic as jumping at the sight of that snow leopard rushing at Graham. All this supports Joseph LeDoux's claim in *The Emotional Brain*, "Much of what the brain does during an emotion occurs outside of conscious awareness." This is great news if you do not want to change how you express your emotions. But you must stop reading now.

Even though how we express our emotions outwardly has become automatic and fast, operating below the level of our awareness, we can take responsibility and relearn how to express our emotions, just as we would relearn how to type, were the layout of the keyboard changed. Every one of us can relearn how to express our emotions because our brains can relearn.

How much can we change? (part two)

We have to engage our inward emotions, outward responses, and the gap in between. We cannot change in the moment. The outward expression of our emotions in the moment has usually become as fast, automatic, and subconscious as typing or jumping at the onrush of a snow leopard. In the moment is too late.

If I may be permitted to speak metaphorically of the emotional brain and thinking brain, the emotional brain, in the moment, exerts greater influence than the thinking brain. Joseph LeDoux says this allows "emotional arousal to dominate and control thinking." His book explains why. This means our emotions all too easily disrupt, overpower, overwhelm, and bump thinking aside.

Here are two reasons why talk of an emotional and thinking brain is inaccurate except as a metaphor. One, as mentioned in chapter 2, our emotions are a form of thinking and communication, just a different kind; two, in the brain everything is connected so that we can not separate emotion from reason. Nothing inside our brains corresponds to our dualistic thinking about emotion and reason.

If the battle is not fought in the moment, when is it fought? It is fought ahead of time by strategizing. Permit me to anticipate what I will say in chapter 11. First, decide what the desired change in behavior will look like; be specific about it. Suppose you do not want to yell at anyone anymore when you get angry. So you tell yourself over and over you will not yell when you get angry. But self-talk is not enough. You also have to work at not yelling. Over time, your emotions and behavior will align with this developing core value. Do not forget to measure change in months, not days and weeks.

This means that down the road, when you yell, your core value, growing stronger, is going to make you suffer guilt for yelling. This is a good thing, even if you feel miserable. Remind yourself that once you have been made to suffer for a couple minutes the horrible guilty feeling will go away. Yes, it is true, your core value and emotion, working together as your friend, are masochistic. Just so you know not to go against your own values, they want you to wallow in misery. Hope you are smiling! All this means, be patient with yourself and extend to yourself lots of self-compassion when you fail. Your heart is in the right place and so, go easy on yourself when you fall flat on your face.

Since you do not want to yell at anyone when you get angry, plan an exit strategy for when you sense your anger building and you are about to yell. Walk away from the situation for as long as it takes to cool down. Figure out what leaving will look like before you start yelling. Deep, long, slow breathing for several minutes can also be one component of your plan. There is also vigorous exercise or taking the dog for a walk. You still have to address why you got angry (chapter 5), and there will be a time for that. Right now, your goal is not to yell.

For sure, you should eventually come to a place where you do what is right for its own sake and not because of fear of punishment or expectation of reward. But if that has not yet happened, consider giving yourself a fun little reward when you succeed in not yelling when you get angry. Fill your successes with joy (chapter 17). Consistent victories will make future encounters with your proneness to yell easier.

Thankfully, as your new way of expressing your emotions grows stronger, that old way will weaken. Unfortunately, the way you formerly programmed yourself to yell when you got angry, that (neural) pathway in your brain will always be part of you. That means you will always have to be vigilant so as not to slide back into old ways, especially when you are exhausted and emotionally drained.

This, to my mind, is how success looks as you walk a path of emotional health and change how you outwardly express anger. Suppose that, prior to desiring change, you yelled at someone once a day. In the first month on this new path, you yell twenty times; the next month, ten; and the month after that, five. After six or seven months of constant, vigilant, and repetitive reinforcement of core values and outward behavior, you are down to two or three times per year. This is awesome success. Getting the number down to zero may be unlikely, especially since your former programming will always be part of you. And since you are no longer making excuses or blaming others, you take full responsibility when you yell, and you sincerely ask for forgiveness. Those who love you will be so incredibly joy-filled about how you are no longer constantly yelling but expressing your anger in more constructive ways. Those who love you will be quicker to forgive than you are to ask for forgiveness!

Demon-theory of emotions

Fury possesses him, he shoves her to the floor, and he forces himself on her sexually. Terrified, she breaks free and runs into the bathroom. He stands before the locked door and pleads for forgiveness, "Honey, I couldn't help myself. An evil spirit provoked me."

It matters not to me whether demons exist. I have not witnessed any evil not due entirely to human cause and agency. And more importantly, we remove human responsibility when we appeal to evil spirits to explain human behavior. I cannot be part of any theology, mythology, or superstition that results in me taking less than full responsibility for what I think, do, and how I feel. Except when it comes to eating ice cream, the words "I couldn't help myself" have no place in my life. I cannot find one verse in the New Testament that leads me to give a demon-theory of emotions any respect.

Unfortunately, a demon-theory of emotions is still all too common in most cultures and religions. It may be found in 1 Samuel 18:10–12 and 19:9–10 in the Hebrew Bible. A demon-theory of emotions is rooted in animism. An evil spirit can dwell in a tree, a mountain, or an emotion. But in precisely the same way that all my toes are my toes, so all my emotions are my emotions. This means, when I get angry, some evil spirit, real or imagined, had nothing to do with it.

I am free to shoulder the burden of responsibility for my life and stop making excuses or shift blame for how I manage and express my emotions. To paraphrase Jim Collins from *Great by Choice*, do I want to build a life that encourages me to shift responsibility, to hold myself less than fully responsible for my choices, and not be ethically accountable for the consequences of my actions?

7

Keep Your Heart with All Vigilance

Paul traveled to Jerusalem to deliver a collection of money to the believers and passed near Ephesus. He called the church leadership to him and said, "Give earnest attention to yourselves and all the flock" (Acts 20:28). For Paul, care for others began with diligent attention to oneself. From his letters, we see how he learned this lesson at considerable cost and pain, to himself and others.

Neglect of self-care and the consequences

A couple years earlier, Paul wrote 1 Corinthians from Ephesus. He had been told some folks in the church at Corinth were unenthusiastic about him and his leadership. He addressed the matter in a concerned, not desperate manner. At the letter's end, he informed the Corinthians of his travel itinerary. He wished to remain at Ephesus until late spring and then cross over into Europe. After visiting the churches in Macedonia over the summer, he would head south to Corinth and perhaps stay the winter. He had no idea where he would go the following year but hoped for their support. Paul added that if his assistant Timothy showed up, be sweet to him (1 Corinthians 16:5–11).

No one knows what happened next, but we have cause and effect. Something compelled Paul to change his announced plans. I speculate Timothy got to Corinth and saw how deplorable things were. He took the faster but more dangerous sea route across the Aegean Sea to tell Paul at Ephesus. That is my guess. This is not: Paul went straight to Corinth, instead of going to Macedonia as he said earlier.

Paul described this visit to the church in Corinth as painful. From 2 Corinthians 1–2, we glimpse what happened. The apostle quarreled with someone; it was personal, nasty, and bitter. Looking back later, Paul admitted he inflicted misery on this individual, and this individual dished it out to him. Things were tense when he arrived. His presence only made things divisive and volatile, for that individual, the church, and himself. Paul left Corinth with the enmity and dissension unresolved but said he would return after going up to Macedonia. However, when he got to Macedonia he changed his mind. Instead of going back to Corinth, he went to Ephesus.

Before departing Macedonia, Paul wrote another letter to the Corinthians and placed it into the heart of Titus. Looking back later, he described his state of mind when he wrote this now lost letter. He was distraught by overwhelming turmoil, anguish of heart, and wretched despair. And because turmoil, anguish, and despair effortlessly transfigure into explosive rage, he scrubbed the Corinthian believers with unhygienic, acid words. It does not surprise me he regretted sending the letter after writing it (did Paul later order it destroyed?). Paul and Titus separated in Macedonia, but before they did, they agreed Titus would go to Corinth, deliver the letter, and then retrace his steps and meet up with Paul at Troas.

After a stay at Ephesus, Paul returned to Troas. When he got there, he found a wide-open door for ministry, but he was agitated, anxious, afraid, impatient, and restless. He could not find Titus, and so he crossed the Bosporus into Europe. There was one road, and I suppose Paul thought he would run into Titus coming from the other direction. They eventually rendezvoused in Macedonia, and Titus reported how the majority in the church at Corinth took Paul's side. But a minority continued to question Paul's leadership. They accused Paul

- of saying one thing and doing something else;
- of being a coward and running away from his problems;
- of making decisions according to human standards and not by God's standards;
- of inconsistent character, acting one way at Corinth and otherwise when not there.

This may be the last time things are harmonious between Paul and the church. For in the year following these events, their relationship disintegrated to the breaking point and possibly beyond. For one piece of evidence suggests the Corinthian church did not contribute to the collection Paul raised for Jerusalem. And if they did not, they meant for Paul to take it personally.

During this extended period of ministry in Greece, Macedonia, and Asia, Paul did not walk the teaching he would later give to the church leadership of Ephesus, "Give earnest attention to yourselves." Make no mistake, Paul gave earnest attention to himself, but it was the selfish, narcissistic, all-about-me kind; he let himself get in the way of leading. Because he did not practice self-care on the side of life and light and love, he sowed anguish, turmoil, and strife in the lives of others, and reaped a harvest of disorder, discouragement, recklessness, and weariness in his own. 2 Corinthians 1–2 is clear, Paul was a mess.

There is more. We have no trustworthy idea what or when it befell Paul, but around the time of writing 1 Corinthians, something so utterly beyond his ability to endure overthrew him, and he despaired of life itself. And so, I wonder, did Paul's disciples—like Abraham Lincoln's friends—stand suicide watch, or in Paul's case, martyrdom watch?

Self-care is never a selfish act

For what I am about to say, I return to the obscurity of speculation and guesswork, and I give Paul the benefit of the doubt, although I admit, this can be constructed differently. I conjecture that when Paul was in Macedonia after leaving Corinth on that visit of misery, he opened his eyes wide, or Titus, that invaluable gift, helped him clear away the clouds. Paul became conscious that he was crippled and debilitated in spirit. I imagine he reasoned that were he to go back to Corinth, as he earlier said he would, and faced his problems directly, nothing would have been accomplished. His presence would only have made things worse.

Having neglected to care for himself for so long, Paul needed time to mend if he was going to effectively care for others. If he did not prioritize self-care, he would, as an instrument of Christ's peace, have precious little to offer others except grief and anger. He came to understand the wisdom in Proverbs 4:23, "Keep your heart with all vigilance, for from it flow the springs of life" (NRSV). Proverbs 4:23 anticipates Acts 20:28, "Give earnest attention to yourselves." In *Let Your Life Speak*, Parker Palmer says, "Self-care is never a selfish act—it is simply good stewardship of the only gift I have, the gift I was put on earth to offer others. Anytime we can listen to true self and give it the care it requires, we do it not only for ourselves, but for the many others whose lives we touch."

Benigno Beltran, introduced in chapter 1, lived what Parker Palmer said. More than knowledge and education, more than performance and skills, Benigno Beltran recognized he himself was the greatest gift he had to offer the poor. He says, "I have long since stopped asking what I can do for the people of Smokey Mountain. Now I am asking who I can be for them."

In *Good to Great*, Jim Collins tells the story of Darwin E. Smith who understood well that one's life is a stewardship and worth caring for. Darwin Smith became CEO of Kimberly-Clark in 1971 and, with ferocious resolve and intense drive, led an impressive and stunning transformation of Kimberly-Clark. Jim Collins says Darwin Smith carried no airs of self-importance and never cultivated hero status. He did not let himself get in the way of leading. He had a full life outside the office and enjoyed getting away to his Wisconsin farm. He was committed to self-care and never stopped developing himself. In retirement after twenty years at the helm of Kimberly-Clark, Darwin Smith reflected back, "I never stopped trying to become qualified for the job." That is personal humility, teachability, and self-leadership. I had Darwin Smith's words made into a plaque. It hangs in my office.

Beverly Engel addresses abused women, but her words in *The Emotionally Abused Woman* can speak to all of us, "Because of all your prior conditioning, you may believe that taking care of yourself is a very selfish act. But your highest responsibility is to yourself. When you take care of your own needs first, you will be able to be a genuinely caring, giving person."

"Genuinely" means our giving and caring can be less than sincere. When we neglect ourselves, our love is given with hooks or strings attached. We can turn into what I like to call an emotional vacuum cleaner, sucking in and not giving out. Do not get me wrong, there is nothing wrong with being an emotional vacuum cleaner, on occasion. From walking a path of emotional health, I have learned to stop denying I deeply need to receive love, and there is nothing wrong about this. But my theology growing up told me giving love was enough. Thankfully, I have learned that love is not only about giving, it is also about welcoming and embracing love from another human being who fills my heart. I need and desire lots of physical hugs.

When we do not give earnest attention to ourselves, we can become absorbed and consumed with ourselves. The metaphorical emotional vacuum cleaner does not turn off. In a word, we become narcissistic.

Narcissistic people are ravenous and insatiable in their lust for such things as power, dominance, money, self-gratification, and the spotlight. A swelter'd venom seeps from a hidden fragility and feeds their egotistical drive. They call for unqualified and unconditional loyalty and submission, and for Christian leaders who are narcissistic, this becomes a symbol of spiritual excellence. To challenge their thinking is to attack them. Their favorite pronoun is "I." And when they give, whether to you or God, they give to get. Their generosity is a business investment; they expect a return. The ancient Romans coined a phrase for this, *do ut des*, "I give to get." They cannot express thanks to you, God, or anyone without taking something away from themselves. Narcissism is self-lust; it has nothing to do with love. Just ask anyone who has befriended, worked for, or been married to a narcissistic person.

We carve out time from our full and active lives for the people we love, always. And if we genuinely love ourselves, we will find time to care for ourselves and give ourselves the attention we require. There is nothing selfish or narcissistic about cleaning the inside of the cup, as Jesus described self-care. It is just good stewardship of the most beautiful gift we have to offer others, the gift of ourselves. Self-care is about filling the inside of the cup of our lives with life and light and love, so that, for the people whose lives we touch, we can touch them with love overflowing.

Top up your emotional gas tank

Imagine that our emotions are contained in an emotional gas tank inside us. When our emotional gas tanks are topped up, we feel confident and likable, and we enjoy more upbeat moods. A filled-up emotional gas tank effectively manages grumpy emotions. We can often shorten their duration and escape them faster. With a filled-up emotional gas tank, we work enthusiastically and productively. We have energy and courage to do things we want and need to do. We are more outgoing, taking initiative in relationships rather than waiting passively. We are less selfish and have more genuine compassion and love for others.

But when our emotional gas tanks are drained, we become cranky and moody. We drag our butts around feeling sluggish and mopey. We make horrible listeners and are less able to manage our emotions effectively. We get irritable sooner, and emotions like anger, fear, and sadness get triggered easier, faster, and more intensely. But somehow, even though our emotional gas tanks are empty, we miraculously still have more than enough emotional energy to make everyone around us miserable.

As part of healthy self-care, it is in our best interests as well as those whose lives we touch, to learn how to fill up our emotional gas tanks and not hold back from habitually refilling them. It is also in our best interests not to drive ourselves so hard and fast that we drain our emotional gas tanks faster than we can replenish them.

Switching metaphors, at the 2007 Global Leadership Summit, Bill Hybels said, "It's your job to keep your batteries charged. The cause that you are about and the leaders you lead deserve to have a fully-charged battery in the chest cavity of their leader." Your cause may be your family; they deserve someone with a fully-charged emotional battery. If you are a teacher, your students deserve someone with a fully-charged battery. Regardless of what our cause may be, Bill Hybels is right, it is our responsibility and ours alone to keep our batteries charged. It is responsible stewardship of our lives.

Please take a moment to journal your thoughts on these four questions:

- How full or empty is your emotional gas tank now?
- Why is your emotional gas tank full, empty, or somewhere in between?
- What sorts of things drain you emotionally?
- What sorts of things fill or energize you emotionally?

If you know the sorts of things that drain you emotionally, and if you fill your day or week with too many of those things, you should not be surprised that you get exhausted and fatigued. Having this awareness of how you tick makes life less complicated. But knowledge is not enough.

It goes without saying, it is impossible to eliminate all the things and people from our lives that drain us. But we can manage our schedules so as to reduce in any given day or week our exposure to stuff that drains us. Just as importantly, we can build into our lives more of the sorts of things that fill us up emotionally. I absolutely adore what Barbara L. Fredrickson says in her book *Positivity* about the changes she brought to her life:

> Having learned from my own research, when I vacation these days, I leave papers and e-mail behind and focus on having fun with my family. I also encourage my students and junior colleagues to do the same, which is the opposite of what my own mentors had encouraged. More important, I look for mini-vacations each day—a walk through the arboretum, lunch with a friend, a dance class, or a book to read for fun. I try to balance my entrenched work ethic with a growing play ethic. I find that vacations from my strong need to achieve refueled me and add depth to my life. In an achievement-hungry workplace, my new approach can at times run against the grain and take some resolve to pull off. Even so, I find the fruits so sweet and abundant that there's no going back to my old ways.

Here is some homework. Journal your answers to these questions:

- What might a play ethic look like in your life? (more in chapter 17)
- What mini-vacations can you build into your day?
- Who or what might discourage you from trying to pull this off?

Thin-skinned, resilient people

Do you think being thin-skinned is a disadvantage in life and work? Look up the word in the *Merriam-Webster's Collegiate Dictionary* and you will read that to be thin-skinned is to be "touchy" and "unduly susceptible to criticism and insult." Not just dictionaries. Being thin-skinned is not valued in our world. Thin-skinned people are accused of being delicate and oversensitive. No one is paying you a compliment when you are told, "Aren't you sensitive."

In many movies we enjoy, being tough as nails is praised. Take a Hollywood script. The entire world of the lead character has just been blown away and within a few seconds another character comes alongside and asks, "Are you okay?" How I want the lead character to respond with biting sarcasm, "Of course I'm alright, you blankety-blank, stupid, obtuse, moron. My husband, kids, friends, parents, and pet puppy, they're all dead and the country has been obliterated. But I'm okay!" I kid you not, you can find respectable psychology websites that instruct you how to do thick-skin skincare: don't let others get under your skin; don't take things too personally; memorize and repeat a gazillion times, "Sticks and stones may break my bones, but words will never hurt me."

There was a time in the history of the English language, however, when possessing thick skin was not applauded. Hundreds of years ago, thick-skinned and thick-skulled people tilled the same soil. Both were wafer-thin, shallow, small-brained, lacking awareness.

Nowadays, thick-skinned people are proud of their density. Just like Ke who could vent emotional puke all over her husband and daughter (chapter 4), so being thick-skinned gives people license to dish it out to others, oblivious or uncaring to how their words and behavior are a weapon of hurt. They reason, "I'm thick-skinned and I expect you to take what I dish out. So don't be touchy!" And you are bewildered why the boss is the top reason people resign from their jobs.

Do not forget this, when you dish it back in kind, thick-skinned people will—as surely as pandas eat bamboo—rain trouble down on you and make your life misery. They just do not see it. People with thick skin have armor that is anything but bulletproof. It is thick-skinned people who are brittle, delicate, hypersensitive, and touchy. They, in fact, are the ones who break easily and have to be coddled. So be careful where you step and keep a baby's plastic pacifier in your desk drawer (for them!). Being around thick-skinned people is like giving a cat a bath; be prepared for a bloody scratching. How long can these emotional bricks wallow in duplicity? To the grave.

Thin-skinned people who walk a path of emotional health see the dangers that come from immunizing themselves against emotional discomfort.

Consider what Taylor Swift, an American songwriter and singer, says, "I've never gotten thick skin. If you close yourself off and you get this protective armor, there is a price you pay with that - of not feeling. And feeling is important when you are a songwriter." Feeling is important for you and me too.

There are other advantages that come with having thin skin and walking a path of emotional health. For one, other people will not have to navigate around your negative emotions and grumpy moods because you do not wear your negative emotions on your sleeve. Personally, I never want anyone to feel they have to pick the right time to talk to me or have to pick the right words. I want people to be safe around me. I'm fond of saying, "Just say what's on your mind and we'll figure out later how to say it."

Having thin skin enables you to be passionate about what you believe in. There is absolutely nothing wrong with getting passionately animated and excited about what drives you. Thin-skinned people walking a path of emotional health are in touch with their emotions, core values, and deep longings inside them (chapter 5). They can harness that beneficial energy to be fanatically driven. When they show up, they are present 200 percent. Thin-skinned people walking a path of emotional health make strong team players and strong team leaders. Fully engaged emotionally, they can disagree with ideas, pound the table, not take things personally when their ideas are challenged, get up and march around the room, as they ferociously, intensely, and excitedly debate and argue ideas looking for the best decision and way forward.

Thick-skinned people, on the other hand, are adroit and cunning with one emotion: volatile anger. They wield aggression—the external expression of their inward resentment and rage (chapter 2)—to attack others until they are defeated, compliant, obedient, and submissive to them.

To be sure, walking a path of emotional health and being thin-skinned does not shield you from the effects of abusive behavior of others. Somehow, there is this idea out there that if you are walking a path of emotional health, you will be like an emotional superman or superwoman, and you will not be affected when others treat you poorly. This is not true. Thin-skinned people walking a path of emotional health feel anguish and pain as deeply as anyone else. And sometimes, they feel distressing emotions more, precisely because they choose not to be thick-skinned. Think of this as one side of the coin.

Here is the other side. Sometimes, people walking a path of emotional health and who are thin-skinned, they feel little or nothing at all when others are verbally and emotionally abusive to them. They think to themselves, "I should be upset by that insensitive remark you just said to me. But I'm not!"

But most of all, love finds it hard, if not impossible, to pass through thick skin. This is the reason I choose to be thin-skinned, even though it means a few more tears. I want my compassion, generosity, kindness, thankfulness, and love to flow effortlessly from my heart, through my thin skin, into the heart of another whom I love or whose life I want to touch.

Being thin-skinned means that most everything can affect you emotionally. But even though you are affected emotionally—when you stand under the shower you get wet—you have something that thick-skinned people lack, resilience.

Resilience is a learned ability to get up after you get knocked down. Yes, you get knocked down by the circumstances of life, by the abusive behavior of others, or by tidal waves of misfortune that wash over you. You may stay down for a bit. But you get up. People walking a path of emotional health get up quicker. To be resilient, you have to process your emotions well and harness that emotional energy courageously (chapters 4–6).

In real and practical ways, thin-skinned people walking a path of emotional health are better prepared for everything life throws at them. They become ferocious in endurance, perseverance, and grit, so that, when exposed to the kicks of all the world or those 10,000 obstacles, they grind away and overcome. At the same time, they experience more emotional heartache and agitation, but it does not last.

People having thin skin and walking a path of emotional health get up after getting knocked down, and they often get up stronger, wiser, and better prepared to face the next storm. Like Barbara L. Fredrickson and Darwin Smith, they are humble, teachable, and practice self-care. To learn, they are willing to perform a thorough examination of what happened and why. This learning can be painful, but they know there is something positive to learn from even the most negative and bleak situations. Then they get back in the saddle.

8

Jesus' Sabbath

Touching Those Things That Bring You Joy

BARBARA FREDERICKSON FOUND THE rewards of healthy self-care "so sweet and abundant" she could not go back to old ways (chapter 7). People living a weekly rhythm of Sabbath have similar experiences. Whether you consider yourself a Christian or not, I invite you to consider building into your life the weekly rhythm of Sabbath, as Jesus understood, lived, and taught it. Jesus' Sabbath can benefit anyone.

What is Sabbath rooted in Jesus?

Jesus showed his followers a new way to look at and live the weekly rhythm of Sabbath rest and restoration. In my opinion, there is nothing more vital and delightful for self-care. A key verse from the teaching of Jesus is Mark 2:27:

> Then he said to them, "The Sabbath was given for the benefit of
> the person, not the person for the benefit of the Sabbath."

Jesus said Sabbath was for his disciples. Jesus told his disciples they were to care for themselves one full day every week, so that they could, on the other six days, lay down their lives in love for others. Jesus gave his disciples six days each week to work and serve others; he gave them one full day every week to go to the beach. Sabbath tied to Jesus was not about substituting one kind of work for another. It was not about exchanging secular work for the Lord's work. Jesus never expected Christians would drive themselves to exhaustion by volunteer labor in church work on Sundays.

Jesus' Sabbath has nothing to do with constraints and prohibitions like you cannot play sports, you should not go to movies, you must not go shopping. Any time you find yourself using words like can't, shouldn't, must, and ought, you are far from Jesus' Sabbath. Here we have one fundamental and irreconcilable difference between Jesus' Sabbath and Sabbath in the Hebrew Bible. In the Mosaic Law, Sabbath was about rest and denying yourself (Numbers 29:7). For Jesus, his gift of Sabbath is about rest and *enjoying* yourself! This weekly rhythm of Sabbath rest and restoration is an extension of Jesus himself, the "lord of the Sabbath" (Mark 2:28). Jesus' Sabbath is joy, freedom, and—metaphorical and real—new wine.

Think of it this way. Jesus' Sabbath is about you having one full day every week where you fill your day with things that top up your emotional gas tank or recharge your emotional batteries (chapter 7). My favorite way to think of Sabbath is to imagine having one full day every week where you are free to touch those things that bring you joy.

When we live Jesus' Sabbath, loving ourselves first so we can then love others (chapter 7), sediments of inappropriate selfishness can dissolve. Our love for others becomes less demanding, controlling, and manipulative. With no strings or hooks attached, there is less "I love you so you will love me." Our love for others will not be restrictive. We will not hold back. There will be no sense of sacrifice in our love (chapter 18).

Sabbath in the Hebrew Bible is not Jesus' Sabbath

Living Jesus' Sabbath is not based on the law of Sabbath in the Hebrew Bible, and for one simple reason: Christians are not bound or tied to the law of Moses in the Hebrew Bible, whether in whole or in part. This is clear from Paul's teaching. Within the context of Romans, Romans 6:14 summarizes Paul's argument, "For you are not under law but under grace." The word "law" here means the law of Moses in the Hebrew Bible, in its totality and unity.

For Paul and his Jewish contemporaries, God is one and the Mosaic law is one, and that means, if we are "under law," you have to obey all of it. Paul says as much at Galatians 5:3, "I testify again to every man who gets circumcised, that he is required to perform the entire law." Substitute any of the laws of Moses for circumcision and Paul's point does not change. If you are "under law," you are not free to pick what commandments to perform as though you were hand-picking fruit at the supermarket, "I'll take the laws of Exodus 21 but pass on the laws of Exodus 20." Every individual commandment was part of a unitary whole.

Paul uses an illustration at Romans 7:2–3 to show why believers in Christ are not under the Law of Moses. He says the law of the Hebrew Bible dictated that a married woman is tied to her husband as long as he lives. But if he dies, she is untied and free to remarry. Paul's point is clear even if his allegory isn't quite accurate. In Christ, believers have died to the Mosaic law, and as a result of that death, have been joined to Christ. Dead to the law of Moses, they are no longer bound to obey it. That includes the fourth commandment, the law of Sabbath.

But are not all days the same?

But some Christians have pushed things further and said, "We don't have to live any kind of Sabbath." Two verses from the New Testament are cited to support this claim:

> For one person evaluates one day as more important than another day, but another person evaluates every day to be the same. Let everyone be fully convinced in their own mind. The one who is resolved to observe the day, is resolved to observe it unto the Lord; and the one who eats, eats unto the Lord, for he or she gives thanks to God; and the one who does not eat, does not eat unto the Lord, and yet he or she gives thanks to God (Romans 14:5–6).

How these two verses can serve to support the claim that we do not have to live any kind of Sabbath is found in verse 5. Paul agrees with those who say all days are the same. Accordingly, Paul says if you want to live Sabbath, fine; if you do not, fine. It is totally a matter of indifference whether you do or not. Paul does not mention the Hebrew Bible law of Sabbath, but it is there and implied.

Paul treats the fourth commandment as he treats circumcision in Galatians and Romans. The Hebrew Bible law of circumcision required Jewish parents to circumcise their sons. But for Paul, because we are not under the law of the Hebrew Bible, it is a matter of entire indifference whether parents circumcise their sons. For Paul, it is like coffee and tea. Drink coffee if you want; drink tea if you want. Drinking one or the other will not bring you closer to God or make you more holy. For Paul, circumcise if you want; do not, if you do not want. As he says at Galatians 6:15, "Neither circumcision nor uncircumcision is anything." For Paul, it is a matter of indifference whether you drink coffee or tea, circumcise or not.

The same goes for the Hebrew Bible law of Sabbath. Believers are free to do it or not do it, just as they are free to drink coffee or tea. For Paul, observing the fourth commandment is a matter of indifference. Mind you, Paul does get worked up when Christians start thinking that circumcision or obedience to the fourth commandment does matter for pleasing God.

I suggest that what Paul says in Romans 14 concerns the fourth commandment and does not address how Jesus lived Sabbath and how Jesus wants us to live it. Whether Paul himself lived a weekly rhythm of Sabbath is irrelevant. From his letters we do not know one way or the other. Were I to guess, I would guess Paul did not live the weekly rhythm of Jesus' Sabbath. Because if he did, I doubt he would have made such a mess of things at Corinth (chapter 7). What is valuable for us is how we see Jesus living Sabbath. And what we see in the Gospels is Jesus and his disciples living a weekly rhythm of Sabbath rest and restoration as a way of life.

But, and this is crucial, what we do not see is Jesus and his disciples living Sabbath in accordance with the Hebrew Bible law of Sabbath. In fact, at Mark 2:23–28 and at its parallel, Matthew 12:1–8, we see the disciples harvesting grain on the Sabbath, something forbidden as sin at Exodus 34:21. The Pharisees had the law of Moses on their side, but Jesus sided with his disciples! And the reason Jesus defended his disciples' breaking the Hebrew Bible law of Sabbath is rooted in how Jesus himself understood, lived, and taught it.

Jesus' Sabbath

The key is Mark 2:28. Keep in mind that when Jesus speaks of "the Son of Man" he is talking about himself. The verse reads, "So then, the Son of Man is lord even of the Sabbath" (Mark 2:28).

For Jesus, the question was, are his disciples to live Sabbath aligned to the Hebrew Bible law of Sabbath, or is there another way? For Jesus, there was another way, and this other way was an extension of Jesus (recall how leadership extends a person's character). As lord of the Sabbath, Jesus told his followers what they could and could not do. No longer were Jesus' disciples to go to the fourth commandment to find rest. They were to go to Jesus. After all, Jesus said:

> Come to me all of you who are driving yourselves to exhaustion and carrying heavy burdens, and I'll give you rest from your toils. Take my yoke upon you and learn from me, for I'm gentle and humble to the very core of my being, and you'll find rest for yourselves; For my yoke is easy, and my burden is light (Matthew 11:28–30).

There is no better way to experience Jesus' rest than to live Jesus' Sabbath.

Lily of the field people

Jesus said, "Why are you anxious about clothing? Take a lesson from the lilies of the field how they grow; they neither toil nor spin" (Matthew 6:28). There is something here that can help us appreciate what Jesus' Sabbath is about. I suggest—in a fun sort of way—that Jesus is quite okay with people being "lily of the field" people one day each week, that is, people who "neither toil nor spin."

Luke 1:78-79 is another passage helpful for understanding Jesus' Sabbath:

> On account of the affections of mercy of our God,
> through which the dawn from on high will come to us,
> to shine upon those who sit in darkness and death's shadow,
> to guide our feet in the path of peace.

The word "affections" literally means the inner parts of the body, such as the intestines. A good English translation of the Greek word might be "guts." Luke uses the word this way when he describes how Judas "fell headlong, burst open in the middle, and all his guts gushed out" (Acts 1:18). It is the literal sense that helps us see what Luke was driving at in Luke 1. It is because we feel emotion with deep intensity in the core of our bodies that the Greek word came to carry the sense of "intense emotion" or "emotion that comes from deep inside a person."

The word "affections" in verse 78 can refer to any kind of intense emotion that flows from deep inside a person. But across the New Testament, as here at Luke 1:78, the word is always used to refer to the deep and intense emotions of empathy, mercy, and love. Luke invited his readers to imagine that from the depths of God's being flows an intense emotion of mercy toward "those who sit in darkness and death's shadow," and, by extension, toward anyone who is in need of a touch of love and mercy. So permit me to ask two questions:

- Do you desire to be touched by this kind of intense emotion of love?
- Would you like to be a person who touches others with this kind of intense love?

If you answer yes, then I invite you, whether you are a Christian or not, to build into your life time for emotional refreshing, for touching those things that bring you joy, for living Jesus' Sabbath.

Before we look at possible applications, I invite you to take a few moments to journal your thoughts on these questions: how might Sabbath look in your life? What obstacles are presently in your life that might get in the way of living this Sabbath?

When we understand Sabbath as Jesus understood, lived, and taught it, we see that we have freedom to take one full day each week for paying earnest attention to ourselves, to rest, to fill our day with things that replenish and energize us, to touch those things that bring us joy.

Implementing Jesus' Sabbath

I can guess why Jesus did not give practical guidance on how to live his Sabbath. Jesus did not want followers who were like marionette puppets dangling at the end of strings. He gave values and principles and had confidence people could take responsibility, plug in their brains, think for themselves, and figure things out. Here are some ideas to get you thinking about how you might live a weekly rhythm of Sabbath rooted in Jesus:

1. Commit to one full day each week, not two half days. Make one full day non-negotiable. Your Sabbath does not have to be Sunday; it does not have to go from sundown to sundown; it does not have to be the same day every week. Avoid saving up Sabbaths the way we bank holidays at work. Creativity, determination, flexibility, and teamwork will always be welcomed as you strive to implement Jesus' Sabbath in your life.

2. Find a person with whom you can share your journey. Make no mistake, living Jesus' Sabbath will be challenging to implement. There is much in your life and world that is going to scream at you as you attempt your first steps. You do not want to go it alone.

3. It will take time to figure out what energizes you and fills you up emotionally. Remember, Jesus' Sabbath is about you touching those things that bring you joy. Experiment. Likewise, it will take time to figure out the sorts of things that exhaust and drain you. There will be activities you will want to say "no" to on your Sabbath.

4. We work to repair and improve everything, and sometimes we feel overwhelmed by all we need to fix in our lives: our bodies, our character flaws, grades, jobs, leadership, likeability, marriages, parenting, and relationships. The list seems endless. Of course, bettering ourselves is part of what it means to be human, and its opposite, stagnation, leaves us like a neighbor's yard overgrown with weeds. We do not want to go there. For what I am about to say, I am sure that some might think I am a few sandwiches short of a picnic, but why not consider your Sabbath as a day to take a rest from working to fix your life. Here's why:

To be fully present we need to be fully absent

This principle is, in part, what Jesus' Sabbath is about, and it applies to just about every area of our lives, including working to fix ourselves.

If I am going to be one hundred percent fully present emotionally, mentally, and socially when I show up at the office at the beginning of my week, I need one full day every week, my Sabbath, where I am one hundred percent mentally, emotionally, socially, and physically absent from work. To be sure, we need to discipline ourselves to regularly stop and reflect on what is going on at work, but Sabbath is not the day for that. Jesus' Sabbath means being absent.

If, prior to my Sabbath, I find my brain racing about something at work, I know that if I am not proactive, my mind will race at 150 kilometers per hour on my day to touch those things that bring me joy. Ruminating about that problem will sap my energy. This is what I do. If there is anything I can do to work the issue prior to my Sabbath, I try to do it. But that is not always possible and so I thoroughly journal everything I am thinking and feeling. That usually works to slow my brain down so that the issue does not devour me on my Sabbath. I want to protect my Sabbath as a day of rest, restoration, and fun. To be fully present, I need to be fully absent.

You know you are on the right track when you wake up the morning after your Sabbath well-rested and ready to go. After all, Sabbath is about rest and refreshment. It is easy for clergy to live Jesus' Sabbath. They can usually take one full day as their Sabbath and instruct their congregations about the importance of boundaries, and why it is a good idea, unless a real emergency, to leave them alone. But laypeople need Jesus' Sabbath too. If they wake up Monday morning tired and frazzled from church involvement on the weekend, they need to re-examine their lifestyle. As I said, it is not what Jesus intends. Part of my mentoring of people is walking beside them as they try to figure out and implement Sabbath so that they too can touch those things that bring them joy.

Benefits of living Jesus' Sabbath

Living Jesus' Sabbath flings the door wide open for living a more ethical life. When our emotional gas tanks are low, we are vulnerable. We are susceptible to violating our core values and integrity. And when we cross the line, we end up dragging ourselves and others down into abuse, compromise, darkness, grief, regret, inappropriate selfishness, and exploitation for our own personal gratification. When we push ourselves too hard and do not rest and replenish ourselves, we do not take care to fully think about what we are doing to ourselves and others. Nor do we think about the consequences of our contemplated actions.

Walking a path of emotional health is not only about managing emotions like anger, fear, sadness, and shame (chapters 10–14). It is also about encouraging positive emotions like empathy, gratitude, joy, and serenity in our life (chapters 17–18). And living Jesus' Sabbath—having one day every week for topping up our emotional gas tanks and touching those things that bring us joy—promotes positive emotions. Rest and joy are inseparable.

Part of life is problem solving. If I am only seventy-five percent present at the office, I will not have the emotional energy I need to intentionally insert myself into a problem and manage it effectively toward a solution. If I am only three-quarters present, I will not listen as carefully as I need to listen to establish the facts. I might make things worse by delaying, downplaying, or exaggerating the issue. Living Jesus' Sabbath allows me to top up my emotional gas tank so I have the emotional energy I need. And by fully disengaging from the problem for a day, I benefit from being able to get a more realistic perspective on things. Taking a break from a problem helps me see how big or small the problem really is. Without a Sabbath break, little problems too often get exaggerated as big problems.

Living Jesus' Sabbath also helps reduce anxiety and stress. Although Marcus Buckingham is not talking about Sabbath in *The One Thing You Need to Know*, what he says fits with living biblical Sabbath rooted in Jesus:

> The best way to succeed is through a disciplined process of stress and recovery. Stress itself is not the enemy we typically think it is. Uninterrupted stress is. So look at your life as a series of sprints, they say, rather than a marathon. Impose on your life a set of routines that allow you to stress yourself, then recover, stress, then recover, and you will find out that, over time, your capacity, your resilience, and your energy will all expand.

Living the weekly rhythm of Sabbath is an excellent routine for rest and recovery for everyone. We can reduce stress, build resilience, and run well the other six days without burning out.

When people get run down and exhausted, their job satisfaction all but evaporates. They complain and feel like bailing out. They see the bad side of everything and everyone and then exaggerate the bad. When a person's emotional gas tank is empty and they complain to me about how much they hate their job, I never take their word for it. I want to know how they feel about their job when their emotional gas tank is topped up. If they still hate their job, then something is there. If you enjoy what you do and want to keep enjoying it, be proactive about self-care and live Jesus' Sabbath.

As precious as Sabbath is, it is not enough; there are six other days too. To them we now turn.

9

Living inside Boundaries

IN HIS *IT WORKED for Me*, Colin Powell described busy leaders who "just can't ever let it go." They arrive early to the office, work late, and show up on weekends. This forces their subordinates to be there when they are there, so they appear as committed as their boss. Colin Powell said these leaders created more work to fill the time, and—this is so true—"most of it was make-work, anything but necessary or important."

As a senior leader, Colin Powell worked with the highest personal and professional standards, and that meant, for one thing, never creating work for anyone that was not absolutely necessary. When necessary, he expected his colleagues to burn the midnight oil. But when not, he wanted them to have a full life outside work and put in normal hours. Colin Powell said, "I am paying them for the quality of their work, not for the hours they work. That kind of environment has always produced the best results for me." He led by example. On weekends he found joy tinkering with old Volvos at home.

This "just can't ever let it go" pattern of overwork, workaholism, and long hours is widespread and esteemed across the globe. It has always been respected in church cultures. Take a young, unmarried woman. She could live in Taoyuan, Taiwan or Toronto, Canada; it does not matter. She has a pastor boyfriend. He has little time for her because he is "giving it all to God." When she asks for time, he says, "Babe, you have to understand." But does she?

Sometimes, long hours are required. Performance and productivity are not adversely affected over the short-haul. But over the long-haul, this "just can't ever let it go" environment of overwork, workaholism, and long hours does not produce, as Colin Powell pointed out, the best results. It also takes a humongous toll on health and relationships.

I may be willing to concede there is one person in 200 who is the exception here. Maybe. But when you dig below the surface into the lives of workaholics, you will find that, despite the image they project, their workaholism is an addiction (chapter 4), and they are not any more productive than those who put in normal work hours over the long-haul. And some workaholics get in two rounds of golf every week and then blame long work hours for their second divorce.

I can make the case that when we overwork over the long-haul, we are less productive. To understand how this is so, recall my principle, to be fully present we need to be fully absent (chapter 8). Or consider my metaphor of a topped up emotional gas tank or Bill Hybels' fully-charged battery (chapter 7).

I leave to one side body weight, eating habits, physical fitness, and sleep patterns, even though each of these powerfully shapes how and why we feel the way we do on a daily basis. These vital factors regulate the amount of beneficial emotional energy available to us for moving forward with the life we want to live and for responding to everything life throws at us.

Some people take their emotional energy and spread it over a normal work week. They work at peak levels of excellence, productivity, and performance. Fanatically driven, they are fully engaged emotionally (chapter 7). Other people take the same quantity of emotional energy and spread it over longer hours and longer weeks. They are physically at work all the time but only give it seventy-five percent, sometimes less.

Suppose you need a real estate agent. Would you want a real estate agent who takes on too many clients, does not have the time for you that you feel you reasonably need, and when you are with her, she pressures you to buy every house you enter? Or suppose you need a lawyer. For lawyers to do their jobs effectively and proficiently, they need an alert mind and an eye for detail. But when your lawyer is fatigued and exhausted from overwork and long hours, things will always get missed. Is that the kind of lawyer you want, someone fatigued and exhausted, and likely to miss things in your account?

When "giving it all to God" dishonors God

Some religious leaders came down from Jerusalem to Galilee and started hanging out with Jesus. Maybe these Pharisees and experts in the law did not quite see eye-to-eye with their colleagues who had earlier investigated Jesus and concluded he was possessed by Beelzeboul, the ruler of demons. They were with Jesus, and before long they saw Jesus' disciples eating without first ceremonially washing their hands. So they asked Jesus why his disciples did not live their lives aligned to the "tradition of the elders."

They knew that hand washing was not required by the Law of Moses. But they put their tradition on a pedestal and expected others to measure up to their standards of purity. Jesus, of course, was not against washing hands before a meal. Sorry kids. But, as we shall see, living by the "tradition of the elders" was a place Jesus was not willing to go. Jesus could not turn the other cheek or adapt his behavior so as not to offend.

When we look at things through the eyes of the religious leaders, we see they were rabid about obeying the law of Moses. In their zeal, they took steps to ensure they did not come remotely close to transgressing one law (not quite accurate, but for the sake of argument). And so they built a fence around the Law, what came to be called the "tradition of the elders." It is easy to see how this fence worked. Take the law of Sabbath. This law prohibited work on the Sabbath. But so as to not come close to violating the commandment, the Pharisees together with other groups cut from the same cloth dreamed up a mishmash of traditions about what could not be done on Sabbath. For example, you cannot talk about work, you cannot walk more than about 450 meters; you cannot wear perfume. The list went on, beyond the point of nausea.

This "tradition of the elders" mentality is with us today. It goes like this, "For sure, abstinence from alcohol is not taught in the Bible. But if you really want to please God, you should not drink alcohol." That "but" is always the butt kicker. Everything after it takes believers far from Jesus, as we will see presently. Whether in the first or twenty-first century, pharisaic people are forever keeping an eye on what others are doing, comparing them against their own standards, and then judging and condemning them accordingly.

Jesus does not walk away. He went right at them:

> Correctly did Isaiah prophesy about you, you fakes! As it is written, 'This people honors me with their lips; but their heart is far away from me. They worship me, but it's just a pathetic waste of time, serving up teachings that are just human commandments' (Mark 7:6–7).

For Jesus, they had to decide. They could hold in their hands the commandment of God or their human tradition. They could not have both. They chose human tradition and washed their hands of what God valued. And in the eyes of Jesus, it was all a pathetic waste of time. To drive the point home, Jesus said their human traditions were shallow lip service:

> "You absolutely have to uphold your tradition, and so you masterfully ignore the commandment of God!" For Moses said, "Honor your father and your mother," and "The one who speaks evil of father and mother shall surely be put to death." But you

say, "If a person tells his father or mother, 'Whatever help you might have received from me is corban, that is, a gift given to God,' then you no longer allow him to do anything for his father or mother, with the result that you annul the word of God for the sake of your tradition which you hand down. And you do many similar things just like these" (Mark 7:9–13).

Jesus uses the fifth commandment, honor your father and your mother. He contrasts the command of God with the human tradition of the Pharisees. Instead of encouraging the son to care for his parents in their old age, the Pharisees pushed the son to tell his parents, "Whatever help and support you might have expected from me when you grow old, don't count on it. I am giving it all to God." Like that girl's boyfriend, and just like Selena's parents (chapter 5), this son was giving it all to God. But Jesus condemned their give-it-all-to-God mentality as a pathetic waste of time that had nothing to do with God.

This workaholic approach to work and ministry, manifested through long hours, burning out, overextending oneself, or giving it all to God, has been a core value in religion forever. It has sown the wind and reaped a whirlwind of anguish, distress, and destruction in the lives of countless neglected children.

Who is your Jethro?

The people of Israel camp at Sinai and Moses sits as judge for the people. Moses' father-in-law sees what's going on and asks Moses, "What in the world, son, do you think you're doing? Why are you sitting here all by yourself while all the people stand around from sunrise to sunset?" There is nothing wrong with showing up, being fully present, busting your butt, and giving it your all, full of passion, energy, and grit determination. But Moses is overworking, putting in too many hours, doing too much. Something is out of joint.

Rather predictably, Jethro gives Moses some practical advice to put sanity back into his life so he can stop overextending himself. But had Moses stopped and plugged in his brain, he would have known exactly what Jethro was going to tell him. But for whatever reason, Moses does not slow down. He does not act wisely. Moses is his own worst enemy. He needs a Jethro to remind him to live within boundaries and limits.

Geri Scazzero, as she tells her story in *The Emotionally Healthy Woman*, asked herself the same question Jethro asked Moses, and when she cleared away the clouds, she saw that there was some dark and ugly stuff inside her that needed her attention. It was not that she was a bad person. But like us, clutter in her inner life was shaping how she lived and the choices she made. And up until that moment, Geri Scazzero was afraid to go inside for fear of what she might see. So, I wonder what Moses might have been afraid to face. What was down there inside rooms in his heart that drove him to work too much? We get a partial answer in the next verses:

> Moses said to his father-in-law, "Because the people come to me to inquire of God. When they have a dispute, they come to me and I decide between one person and another, and I make known to them the statutes and instructions of God" (Exodus 18:15–16, NRSV).

Can you hear yourself in Moses' words? Moses is basically saying, "Get off my back, dad, it's not my fault. Everyone has problems and they keep coming to me. There is so much need and I can't turn away." There is more. Moses got himself into a place where he believed God wanted him to burn out and martyr himself.

Geri Scazzero relates a story about a man who once told her, "I'll have plenty of time to rest in heaven. For now, I'll work as long and as hard as I can." On the surface, this sounds so saintly and holy. But like Moses, he deceived himself into thinking that this lifestyle of "burn out for Jesus" was a way of life that honored God.

Jethro sees through Moses' self-deception and refuses to play along. Make no mistake, it is self-deception:

> Moses' father-in-law said to him, "What you are doing is not good. You will surely wear yourself out, both you and these people with you. For the task is too heavy for you; you cannot do it alone" (Exodus 18:17–18, NRSV).

As we will see when we come to verses 19–20, Jethro does not question Moses' calling. He agrees with Moses: "Yes, Moses, I affirm your calling from God. Don't quit! Don't bail out!" But where Jethro disagrees with Moses is in challenging Moses' belief that God wants him to put in long hours and burn out. Jethro challenges Moses' belief he is actually doing anyone any good by working too much and wearing himself out. In fact, Moses is doing more harm than good by not living within boundaries.

Can't I do all things through Christ who strengthens me?

Someone who knows their Bible might push back, but did not the Apostle Paul himself say, "I can do all things through him who empowers me" (Philippians 4:13)? And if this someone can read Greek, they can point out that Paul emphasizes "all things." Why should I care about long hours, burning myself out, and self-care, when I have this insanely fantastic promise that I have divine power to do all things?

When we tether Philippians 4:13 to its context in Philippians 4, we see that the verse most assuredly does not teach that we have unlimited resources to do all things through divine power. When we respect the context, we see Paul saying that in all circumstances, whether he has little money and goes hungry, or has plenty of money and is well-fed, he is okay and fine. He is content because he is in Christ who strengthens him. Because Christ provides for his needs (see verse 19), Paul is content (see verse 11) and can keep his head above water, whether life's circumstances favor him or grind him down. Philippians 4:13 does not say we are superheroes, able to do all things with Christ's power.

It will be easier for you

Jethro knows that people who burn out, overwork, and overextend themselves do not think straight. They make dumb decisions. Our collective wisdom says the same: do not trust decisions made when exhausted.

Where people burn out, overwork, and overextend themselves, not working within healthy boundaries, everyone gets to comparing themselves with everyone else. Resentment and unhealthy competitiveness set in. A leader putting in long hours reasons, "If I'm going to burn out and sacrifice, I expect the same from you!" I like how Matt Ridley in *Nature via Nurture* responds to this logical lunacy, "The faster you run, the more the world moves with you and the less you make progress." Colin Powell witnessed the same in busy leaders. Or if we ask Alice, she might say, "My dear, here we must run as fast as we can, just to stay in place. And if you wish to go anywhere you must run twice as fast as that" (Lewis Carroll). The last thing busy leaders want around them are people who know better and who refuse to play their game.

God never intended for Moses to be over-responsible and deal with all the problems of all the people of Israel. There were things God wanted Moses to do; there were things God did not want him to do. Jethro's role was to help Moses wake up and see through his self-deception. Marcus Buckingham says, "Great leaders rally people to a better future." That is precisely what Jethro was doing for Moses. Jethro then says:

> Now listen to me. I will give you counsel, and God be with you! You should represent the people before God, and you should bring their cases before God; teach them the statutes and instructions and make known to them the way they are to go and the things they are to do (Exodus 18:19–20).

Healthy relationships are the gold standard. Moses had someone who had earned the right to speak truth into his life, someone who could say, "Open your eyes!"

Like Moses, we need a Jethro, someone who loves us and has earned the right to speak truth into our lives and remind us, whether with a gentle nudge or a good metaphorical kick in the butt, to stop putting in long hours and burning out. Take this to heart: the deeper the relationship, the more effective the influence.

Here is the rest of Jethro's advice:

> You should also look for able men among all the people, men who fear God, are trustworthy, and hate dishonest gain; set such men over them as officers over thousands, hundreds, fifties and tens. Let them sit as judges for the people at all times; let them bring every important case to you, but decide every minor case themselves. So it will be easier for you, and they will bear the burden with you. If you do this, and God so commands you, then you will be able to endure, and all these people will go to their home in peace (Exodus 18:21–23, NRSV).

Jethro tells Moses to abandon his reckless, overworking ways and share the load. Thereby he can endure. I wish you would own these words, "It will be easier for you." Then Jethro says, "Let others share the burden." To paraphrase Jethro's words to Moses, "Lighten up and let others." And look who benefits, everyone! Moses gets to lighten up, endure, and not burn out. And people around him are free to live balanced lives. They do not have to be there from sunrise to sunset (mind you, that's not a long day in December in Calgary where I live). Everyone, verse 23 says, "goes to their home in peace" (NRSV). Let me ask, what would your life be like this year if you lived within healthy boundaries and limits?

10

The Experience of Anger

Imagine a conversation between you and yourself:

You:	I'm angry but I don't like feeling angry.
Yourself:	But our anger loves you.
You:	Well, I don't feel loved.
Yourself:	Let me guess, you feel like ripping his head off?
You:	I can start there.
Yourself:	But our anger is our friend.
You:	My friend is going to help me rip his head off?
Yourself:	If you do that, don't blame our anger.
You:	But it's so easy to blame our anger.
Yourself:	Our anger is beneficial energy and a most effective emotional response to —
You:	help me understand and respond to what I'm facing right now.
Yourself:	You've been paying attention!
You:	I want to feel normal.
Yourself:	Our anger is normal. We need it to see, understand, and do what needs doing.
You:	Rip his head off?
Yourself:	No. Focus on what is disturbing us and act.

Since my youth, my head said one thing and my heart another when it came to anger. How I experienced anger was poles apart from what my head told me. I realized anger was not sinful, but I did not see it as my friend, let alone beneficial, constructive, or necessary. I did not grasp that anger can guide me to get to the bottom of why I am angry and help me make decisions for change. I felt my anger was dangerous and unacceptable. The measure my maturity was not to feel the emotion of anger at all. In short, I did not have a healthy tie to my anger and I did not give myself permission to confront and embrace my anger. All I got for this was regret and resentment. These buried emotions inside me generated anxiety, frustration, indecisiveness, and more anger, in room after room in my heart.

When it came to my anger, my head got it right. But make no mistake, lots of people think my head got it wrong. They believe we never have the right to be angry because they think the emotion of anger is bad and destructive. The goal is to be free of anger. The mark of spiritual enlightenment and maturity is ceasing to be angry. And many Christians think the experience of anger is sin and they go to the Bible for support.

Is the emotion of anger sin?

At Galatians 5:17–21, Paul puts anger beside sexual immorality and idolatry in a list of iniquitous, sinful behaviors. He warns his readers that if they do these things, including anger, they will not inherit salvation. Strong words: feel angry and fall away from God's grace; so much for persevering in grace. But I am perplexed by what Paul said. For when he wrote Galatians he was angry, and later, when he wrote 2 Corinthians 10–13, he was, to put it mildly, raving mad. Both letters bleed razor-sharp, vulgar sarcasm oozing from suppressed anger and resentment. Little of this comes across in our English translations of the Greek.

Jesus' teaching in the Sermon on the Mount also aligns anger with sin:

> You have heard that it was said to those of ancient times, "You shall not murder," and "whoever murders will be answerable to the court." But I say to you that everyone who is angry with his brother will be answerable to the court; and whoever says to his brother, "You empty-head," will be answerable to the Jewish high court; and whoever says, "You moron," will be answerable to the hell of fire (Matthew 5:21–22).

You are not alone if you are uncomfortable with what Jesus said about anger and hellfire. Sometime in the second century, someone trained to make manuscripts prepared a new copy of the Gospel of Matthew. He came to this passage and did not like what he saw. And so he added one word in Greek that gets translated "without a cause" in the King James Version. With this addition, Jesus now taught you have nothing to fear so long as you have good reason for your anger. But look out if you do not have a cause.

Separate Matthew 5:21–22 from Jesus' life and it seems he says what that second-century scribe thought he saw in the text before he messed with it. But when we weave this teaching onto the tapestry of Jesus' life, we see Jesus and his disciples getting angry, and Jesus never reprimanding anyone for feeling angry. None of this we expect if Jesus saw the emotion of anger as sin.

The distinction between the internal emotion and its external expression, which I introduced in chapter 2, helps me navigate Matthew 5:21–22, Galatians 5:17–21, and other passages in the New Testament that connect sin to anger. Suppose these passages are talking about behavior that results from what we decide to do with our emotion of anger, behavior that opposes core values like responsibility, love, gentleness, and self-control. That Paul was talking about how we express the emotion of anger fits the context of his letter to the Galatians exceptionally well. A few verses earlier he talked about inappropriate expressions of anger: "But if you bite and devour one another, take care lest you be consumed by one another" (Galatians 5:15). The same goes for Jesus. He focuses on how we express anger in words that can destroy relationships. And he holds out optimism, encouragement, and confidence that anyone can constructively manage and assertively express their anger in love-enhancing ways, accompanied by self-control and responsibility.

Not sin, but should I strive to be anger-free?

Yoda (Frank Oz) taught Luke Skywalker (Mark Hamill) this when Luke was training to be a Jedi. Recall Yoda's last words to Luke in *Star Wars: Return of the Jedi*, "But beware: Anger, fear, aggression - the dark side, are they." And later, Emperor Palpatine told Luke he felt Luke's anger; not a good thing in that galaxy far, far away. Being angry would make Luke more and more the emperor's servant. All Luke needed to do was give in to his anger and his journey toward the dark side would be complete.

Back in our galaxy, Diane has been married twenty years. After years of frustrated and fruitless attempts to get her husband to sit down with her and address problems in their marriage, she just gave up. Diane is still physically present in the marriage, but she has checked out. Having lost respect for him, nothing her husband now says or does triggers her anger anymore. Free of anger, Diane has zero interest in coming to an understanding with her husband on anything.

If you want to be anger-free, follow Diane and learn to be apathetic, detached, and indifferent toward everyone and everything. For if someone or something matters to you, you will be acquainted with anger. Look at what triggered Jesus' anger; you will see what mattered to him. Look at what triggers your anger and you will see what matters to you.

Cain was neither detached nor indifferent (Genesis 4). He and Abel brought offerings to God. God welcomed Abel's offering but spurned his. Maybe Cain did not get the memo of what God wanted. God's behavior provoked his anger. Other emotions often trigger anger, and that is likely what is going on here. God rejected Cain's offering and that sparked his disappointment, frustration, and sadness. These, in turn, ignited anger. All these emotions were involuntary and automatic, occurring with lightning speed.

The only way for Cain to avoid anger was for him to be as caring as a marble statue or like Diane after twenty years of marriage. But Cain cared, and he cared quite decidedly, for he became at least eight out of ten angry when God rejected his offering. Like Cain, we get angry about things we hold close to our heart. We get angry because our anger is soaked with core values about what is dear to us.

For sure, our anger can cloud our thinking and blind our judgment, especially when it is boiling over. Nevertheless, our anger almost always has something important to tell us about what is wrong in a relationship or situation before our eyes. That is why it is in our best interests to admit when we are angry and give ourselves permission to feel anger. Because we get angry about things we care about, it is to our benefit to take hold of our anger (chapter 4), listen to what our anger is telling us (chapter 5), and then courageously work to address what specifically needs our attention (chapter 6). But way too often, we do not want to hear the message our anger is trying to deliver to us. That is why sometimes we deny we are angry, or we attribute the cause of our anger to something other than the real cause.

The impulse toward aggression and revenge in anger

No one is protected from this impulse. It is *"more powerful than all reason,"* Alice Miller says in *Breaking Down the Wall of Silence*. When furious rage rips us apart, every fiber in our bodies pushes us to hit, retaliate, slam doors, throw things, slap, yell, and avenge ourselves. We can become dangerous.

Others of us do not think we have a problem with anger because we barely ever raise our voice or express that impulse toward aggression and revenge in combatively violent ways. We avoid direct conflict, but we are aggressive all the same. It is called passive-aggressive. In *Facing Shame*,

Merle A. Fossum and Marilyn J. Mason tell the story of a woman who was not permitted to express anger growing up. The authors asked her how she expressed her anger toward her parents. Without hesitating, she said, "I married someone they didn't like."

Most people who prefer to avoid direct confrontation when they are angry do not go so far as to marry someone to spite their parents. But at their team meeting, they wholeheartedly support your ideas and then later, behind your back, do everything to undermine you. Others, when angry, withdraw and dish out the silent treatment as their way to inflict pay-back. Or they mope, frown, pout, sulk, make sarcastic remarks, put you down, or withhold expressions of love. So let me ask, are these external expressions of anger that range from slamming doors to the silent treatment, ever healthy and acceptable?

Absalom was a master door slammer. He had fled after killing his step-brother Amnon for Amnon's rape of his sister Tamar (I tell the story in chapter 12). Later, Joab coaxed David to allow Absalom to return. Two years went by and Absalom, back in Jerusalem, was not welcomed by his father. So Absalom repeatedly asked Joab to come to him but Joab refused. The Bible does not zoom in on Absalom's emotions, but I imagine he was frustrated and angry by Joab's refusal to come to him. Joab had a barley field next to Absalom's farm, and so Absalom acted on anger's aggressive impulse and told his slaves to set the field on fire. That got Joab's attention and undoubtedly reinforced in Absalom's brain that aggression and violence work when niceness does not (2 Samuel 14).

Is yelling acceptable in day-to-day relationships?

What went on between Joab and Absalom happens to us. When Absalom spoke, Joab did not listen. Niceness was not working. Have you ever felt you had to yell to be heard? I am sure that is how Absalom felt. But instead of yelling to be heard, he set Joab's field on fire. Likewise, there are times we feel that to be heard, we must set someone's field on fire—metaphorically speaking—and it usually takes the form of yelling. There is a strategic place for yelling on the battlefield. Soldiers under enemy fire are ordered to move forward, something entirely at odds with natural human instinct. Yelling may be necessary to get soldiers moving. But did Absalom have to set Joab's field on fire to get his attention?

Colin Powell believes there is an acceptable place for yelling when angry. To return to *It Worked for Me*, he tells how a sergeant stood across from his desk about to be disciplined for drunk driving. Given the seriousness of the charge, the sergeant was facing reduction in rank and a fine. He groveled, pleading to be let off. He said it would affect his family, were he punished. The logic did not escape Colin Powell. It was the punishment meted out and not the drunk driving that was going to adversely affect the sergeant's family. When Colin Powell heard these words, he was provoked to anger.

Colin Powell admits he got angry because he was at wit's end having to deal with a string of soldiers under his command charged with drunk driving. But his annoyance, exasperation, and frustration at having to waste time dealing with people's criminal recklessness was not the sole reason he got angry. Over his career, Colin Powell developed a clear sense of what a leader and a leadership culture can look like. His book articulates this transformative vision. The sergeant slammed hard into several of Colin Powell's leadership core values. Colin Powell wanted to nurture a leadership culture where leaders solve problems and not manage around them by "burying them, minimizing them, reorganizing around them, [and] softening them." That is precisely what his sergeant did, instead of courageously facing up to them.

Colin Powell also wanted to nurture a leadership culture where leaders did not "blame somewhere outside [their] responsibility." The sergeant was to blame for driving drunk and responsible for the repercussions of his behavior. He should have said as much. But instead, he cowardly and inappropriately blamed Colin Powell for the consequences of driving drunk. In blaming the wrong person, the sergeant was not acting responsibly. This sergeant was not measuring up to Colin Powell's core values about how leaders can lead. It is entirely comprehensible why Colin Powell's anger flared. His anger loved him, was aligned with his core values, and was acting as his friend. His anger rallied to his side to help him make sense of and respond to what he was facing.

Colin Powell describes what transpired next. He "totally lost it." Aroused by anger's aggressive impulse, he stood up, slammed his fist on the desk, and shattered the glass top. The crash was so loud his staff came running in to rescue the sergeant. He confessed that his explosion of emotion felt good. Colin Powell said, "Sometimes my explosions are right and justified," and "I wasn't sorry to let them realize it could happen again." After this, he learned to display "extreme, out-of-my-comfort-zone displeasure without destroying government property."

Earlier in his career, Colin Powell was written up for a "severe temper" that had manifested itself in "a screaming match on a phone with another officer" where he "pretty much lost it." He admits that being written up was a life preserver for him. He says, "I've worked hard over the years to make sure that when I get mad, I get over it quickly and *never* lose control of myself." He confesses a few lapses, "Sometimes I let my temper get the best of me, and I blow up. Leave me alone, stay out of the way, and I'll be back to normal shortly. Don't take it personally; I really just got hung up on the issue. I can't have people around me who go fetal when they get caught on my gun-target line."

Solid advice. When we feel we are going to be overthrown by anger's aggressive impulse, it is not a bad idea to get away and calm our bodies down. That Colin Powell learned to display anger without destroying property is also commendable. That he worked hard to make sure that when he got angry he got over it quickly is too. But the sergeant was not under enemy fire. Unleashing explosive behavior against him will have brought about compliance and put the sergeant on the defensive. But there were lessons the sergeant needed to learn about respect, consideration of others, responsibility, and courage. A collegial, safe environment is far more conducive than an adversarial one for learning.

Colin Powell's behavior got in the way of an effective teaching time. Maybe then the sergeant would have felt the same disappointment Colin Powell felt and had an appropriate dose of healthy guilt for his criminal stupidity. Colin Powell might have been able to align his sergeant to his core values about leadership. But as both look back today, that is not what they remember. What would be remembered is how Colin Powell "totally lost it" and the sergeant needed to be rescued. Could Colin Powell have expressed his anger and communicated how grave things were without surrendering to anger's impulse toward aggression and revenge?

There is more. Colin Powell says that when he loses it, it is the responsibility of those around him to deal with it. He does not want thin-skinned people nearby who "go fetal." In other words, if his leadership team does not respond to his explosions of anger the way he wants, it is their fault. And like his sergeant, Colin Powell wants sympathy: circumstances are to blame when he loses it, whether he is hung up on some issue or has to deal with a string of soldiers charged with drunk driving.

But we are responsible for managing the circumstances of our lives so that we can reduce the number of stressful times when we are overwhelmed. And we are responsible for how we manage and express our anger.

If you decide there is a proper place for yelling at someone, you have Colin Powell in your corner. But for me, except on the battlefield and in other life-threatening circumstances, there is never an appropriate place for yelling. There is, as well, no place for setting someone's field on fire and other forms of explosive, violent behavior. The Bible shows that cruelty expressed Absalom's character as a result of Absalom time after time choosing to express his anger violently. Yes, niceness did not work to get Joab's attention. That is a window into Joab's character. But I cannot imagine there was no other alternative for Absalom other than resorting to violence to get the attention of Joab.

One more example. Despite exhaustion and hunger, Gideon and his 300 men were pursuing two Midianite kings (Judges 8). When they came to Succoth and Penuel on the east side of the Jordan River, Gideon requested food and both towns refused. Those towns were not stupid. They knew that so long as Gideon's enemies were out there, their safety was precarious. Gideon's fight was not their fight. They were telling Gideon, "Please keep us out of it."

Gideon took their refusal as a personal attack. His anger pricked, he told them he would teach them a lesson they would not forget when he returned. Gideon's actions had nothing to do with justice and everything to do with settling scores: you hurt me, I am going to hurt you back, and I am going to enjoy watching you suffer. There are no excuses here: Gideon allowed anger's impulse toward aggression and revenge to cloud his thinking. He chose to be blind to justice and could not compassionately empathize with the difficult situation the families of Succoth and Penuel found themselves in. In not attending to his anger, Gideon irresponsibly gave it open range. Gideon's anger offered him easy rationalizations to justify violence and mobilize him to let slip the dogs of war, which he did ruthlessly and with cold-blooded murder.

When we unleash this impulse toward aggression and revenge inherent in the emotion of anger, it indiscriminately pushes us to abusively hurt others and make them suffer. The more intense our anger, the less stable and self-controlled we are. This impulse in anger cannot go away. But yelling and other forms of violent behavior as expressions of anger can be significantly reduced in our lives. We have to decide that is the path we want to walk. To that we now turn.

11

The Positive Management of Anger

CONSIDERING HOW ANGER WORKS, it is not surprising that a superabundance of psychological and self-help books together with the Bible encourage us to take anger seriously. All aspects of anger call for vigorous attention:

- the internal emotion and its impulse toward aggression and explosive behavior;
- the varieties of external expression; and
- the time-gap between the internal emotion and its external expression.

Becoming anger-free is never the goal. Managing and expressing anger in problem solving ways is.

Our anger is entirely our responsibility

I recommend that each of us create a personally tailored, practical strategy that we can implement to manage and give constructive expression to our anger. This means experimenting and trying different techniques. What works for me may not work for you. Eventually you will build a strategy that works effectively for you.

Your strategy must start with taking responsibility for your anger. This is non-negotiable. You must stop saying you cannot help it when you fly off the handle. You have to stop making excuses. And when you take full responsibility, you open doors for change and growth.

Elkanah was a polygamist, married to Peninnah and Hannah (1 Samuel 1). Elkanah loved Hannah but had little love for Peninnah. He provided dutifully for Peninnah and his lack of love did not stop him from using her for his own gratification as a sex-toy with babies to show for it.

Peninnah knew she could not bite the hand that fed her. And so she took her shame, heartache, and resentment and lashed out in anger at Hannah, who was weaker, vulnerable, and nearby. Peninnah was miserable and she made Hannah suffer. This went on for years with Elkanah little troubled by what was happening.

Peninnah had every right to be furious. She deserved to be treated with honor, appreciation, and respect. There is a place for assigning appropriate blame, and she was not to blame. But here is the metaphorical kick-in-the-head. Even though Peninnah was not at fault, it was her job, and her job alone, to carry the full burden of self-responsibility for what she did with her own anger. I could say the same for Cain (chapter 10).

In the same way, regardless of who or what may trigger our anger, we are responsible for what we do with it. We may have an inherited, genetic predisposition that results in greater susceptibility to our anger getting triggered easier, faster, and more intensely; we are responsible. We may have grown up in a home where we learned some rather nasty ways to express anger; sorry but we are responsible. I know it is hard and it does not seem fair, but

- if we want to scale down yelling and other forms of aggressive behavior as expressions of anger;
- if we want to reduce expressing anger in sneaky, passive-aggressive ways such as holding onto a grudge or withholding affection; or
- if we want to reduce directing our anger inward against ourselves in self-hatred;

then we want to learn to assertively communicate our anger in problem solving ways. It starts with taking responsibility. Beverly Engel took responsibility for her anger and later testified in *Honor Your Anger*, "The positive management of my anger has been one of my greatest accomplishments." Post that on your fridge or your social media.

Take a time-out and regroup

Seneca, the Roman statesman and philosopher, said, "The greatest remedy for anger is delay." The Book of Proverbs says as much. And we saw how Colin Powell learned to walk away when he felt his anger getting the better of him.

David and his 600 men were away and the Amalekites attacked Ziklag where they had been living (1 Samuel 30). They torched Ziklag and took everyone captive, including David's wives. When David and his men returned, they were overcome with sorrow to the point of exhaustion. The Bible says they had no strength to cry. But in their bitterness David's men still had more than enough emotional strength to point the finger at David for the atrocity and set themselves on killing him as a way to avenge themselves.

Please observe the progression. Their intense sadness gave way to corrosive bitterness, then to anger, and then a thirst for revenge. These volatile emotions were generating lots of irrational thinking. But were they asked, I think they would have said their thinking was entirely logical. David was in danger.

David's emotions mirrored his men's. He too was overthrown emotionally and exhausted by sorrow. His emotions were screaming at him to run his men through with a sword. But instead of allowing himself to be carried away by his emotions and act irrationally, erratically, and cruelly, he restrained the impulse toward revenge and aggression in his anger and chose to strengthen himself. He wisely ran away, took a time-out, rested, and regained strength. I want you to remember that restraining anger is not the same as suppressing it. David still needed his anger. Later, with his feet firmly on the ground, and his anger harnessed and now energizing him, he led his men in pursuit of the bad guys to rescue loved ones.

Taking a time-out to regroup can also involve keeping your mouth shut and, as I said in chapter 4, walking away and focusing on something else until you calm down. As part of a time-out and regroup strategy, you can also try journaling your thoughts and emotions.

Reprogramming your brain

I need time-management principles to help me work faster because I have more work before me in any given week than I can attend to. Handle everything once works for me. Today I was unloading the car and I pulled out the lawn dethatcher. It needed to go to the backyard shed. My first inclination was to set it down, finish unloading the car, pick it up later, and take it around back. But handle everything once popped into my mind. Applying Paul Ekman's research from *Emotions Revealed* on "*automatic* appraising mechanisms" in the brain, what happened was this. I did not intentionally rummage inside my brain for handle everything once. Rather, below my conscious awareness, my brain appraised the situation and detected that handle everything once may be useful. My brain pushed it into my awareness, all with lightning speed. I decided to apply handle everything once; I put the dethatcher away without procrastinating. You will see in a moment how this relates to managing anger.

When gripped by intense anger, we are not receptive to thinking rationally in the moment. On account of this, Aaron Ben-Ze'ev, in *The Subtlety of Emotions*, likes the metaphor of a fire drill: students do fire drills so that, if there is a fire and kids panic, they can still get to safety with minimal thinking. Similarly, when our anger rages, we need a fire-drill escape route. Just like my time-management principle, handle everything once, we need one or two principles, already programmed into our brains, that will automatically push into our awareness when we get angry. In the gap between the onslaught of the anger and how we respond, our programmed brain can provide us with a time-out and regroup path. We still have to decide to act on these principles. Here are four examples: time for some deep breathing; no hitting ever; no yelling; go for a walk.

A short, memorable action principle opens for us another path of response as we seek to manage our anger. No one has ever said this will be easy. But the more we act on the short, memorable principle, the more the principle gets programmed and reinforced in our memory and the faster our brain pushes it into consciousness when needed. The key is repeated doing, over and over and over. Come up with a short memorable principle and do it repeatedly as part of your personal strategy for managing and expressing anger. With time, you will be able to reduce unhealthy expressions of anger that get in the way of harnessing the energy of your anger to problem solve.

Speak truth to your anger

King Saul did not speak truth to his anger and this was due, in part, to his insecurities getting the better of him. But earlier in his life, he was obedient to his father, lovingly empathetic and generous, a team-player, and good listener. He valued honor and integrity, and he exhibited restraint and self-control when others attacked his character or his status threatened (1 Samuel 9–11). In the face of injustice, Saul got angry and his anger was the appropriate emotional response. He harnessed anger's beneficial energy and rallied people to stand on the side of justice against oppression. Much about Saul's early life deserves our respect.

But when Samuel summoned the people to anoint him king, Saul hid among the luggage. Given Samuel's words to Saul later, "Though you are little in your own eyes" (1 Samuel 15:17, NRSV), we can infer Saul struggled with insecurities, timidity, fear, and lack of self-confidence. When he became king, these insecurities manifested themselves in arrogance, narcissism, and viciousness.

King Saul appointed David over his army. David led Saul's army in successful campaigns, and so people began singing, "Saul has killed his thousands, and David his ten thousands" (1 Samuel 18:7, NRSV). When Saul heard this, his anger flared. Nothing wrong here, but Saul missed an opportunity to speak truth to his anger. David and he were on the same side, David was out there fighting and one should expect David to slaughter more people, and Saul should have considered the source of the singing: gossips and meddlesome busybodies who liked to compare people.

Earlier Saul had exhibited self-control in the face of criticism. Now he went into meltdown and directed his rage against David. Overwhelmed by insecurities, Saul now had to be the brightest star in his universe. He became a celebrity politician concerned only with his own reputation and grip on power. Saul's toxic competitiveness generated truckloads of jealousy and out-of-control rage. For where there are chronically angry people, there you will find toxically competitive cultures, at home, school, and work.

Saul's earlier love of justice also suffered. He could not endure the truth that the priest Ahimelech had been duped by David's lies and deception. Entirely insecure and consumed by wrath, Saul became estranged from the empathy that characterized his earlier life. Unwilling to speak truth to his anger, he angrily and mercilessly had everyone butchered in the priestly town of Nob (1 Samuel 21–22).

Jesus knew the value of speaking truth to anger. The mother of James and John came to Jesus to ask that her sons sit on his right and left in his kingdom (Matthew 20). When the other disciples heard this, they understandably became angry and directed their anger at James and John. Jesus did not reprimand them for getting angry. Jesus seized the opportunity to speak truth to their misdirected anger, teaching them a lesson about leadership.

What is your anger telling you?

Theodore Isaac Rubin began his *The Angry Book* with words from novelist Joseph Conrad, "There is no rest for a messenger 'til the message is delivered." Fitting words.

We have seen a few of the ways our anger gets triggered. We get angry about what matters to us or when people—or ourselves—do not live up to expectations. We get angry when we are stressed, exhausted, and pulled in too many directions. Our competitiveness, insecurities, fear, and lack of self-confidence trigger anger. Emotions like discouragement, frustration, humiliation, jealousy, resentment, sadness, and shame do too.

Because your anger normally has something to tell you, your strategy for managing it will include taking all the time necessary to explore what triggered your anger (chapter 5). By listening to your anger, you give your anger a voice, exactly what it wants. When you take your anger seriously, your anger no longer gets in the way of love. Rather, as your friend, your anger and love team-up to help you address the issue and make decisions for change.

This does not mean the message is always reliable. After all, when we get angry, our anger looks for words to match how we feel. Suppose Dorothy is virulently angry with her boyfriend, and she says some cruel and nasty things to him. Dorothy hears what she just said and wonders to herself, "Is this what I really think of him?"

For sure, sometimes words said in anger communicate correctly what we believe. Sometimes our anger gets the words right. But just as often our anger does not. We have all said words in anger we did not mean. There is only one way for Dorothy to know for sure whether her words were on or off the mark. As difficult as this can be, she needs to take hold of what she said about her boyfriend and evaluate those harsh words to see if there is any truth in them. And honest or not, what Beverly Engel says in *Honor Your Anger* holds true, "Words said in anger can sever the strongest of ties."

Courage to do what needs doing

At the time of the rebuilding of Jerusalem in the fifth century BCE, the Jewish ruling class was exploiting its own people (Nehemiah 5). They saw nothing wrong with what they were doing and did not care so long as the rich got richer. The people, crushed and abused by the ruling families, had to raise money to pay their taxes. Some sold their children into slavery. Disheartened and disillusioned, they pledged their farms to buy food and avoid starvation. Their properties were soon in the hands of the ruling families. All very legal, so the ruling families could still worship at the temple, pay their tithes with a clean conscience, and have priests pronounce blessings over them.

In their helplessness, bitterness, and despair, the people cried out. Nehemiah heard their complaints, and because emotions are contagious, Nehemiah probably felt their anxiety, despair, and fear. Then his anger ignited. He did not confess his anger as a sin or strive to be anger-free. Nehemiah went away, took a time-out, and in the company of his anger and the facts, he planned. At the risk of his own life, he confronted the ruling families. I bet he was scared to death, but he saddled up anyway. Nehemiah publicly exposed the abusive and exploitive behavior of the ruling families and rallied the people. Faced with a monstrous, unhappy mob and the determination of one angry leader, the ruling families caved in.

In *Honor Your Anger*, Beverly Engel describes this kind of anger:

> Anger can create powerful changes in the world. It can be a catalyst for bringing atrocities to light, stamping out injustices, and create new structures and systems to replace those that are corrupt and inadequate. Anger can empower those who have been tyrannized or victimized, imbuing them to stand up to their oppressors.

We can harness anger's emotional energy for positive outcomes. We do this by listening thoroughly to what our anger is trying to tell us. Most often an issue that needs our attention will unfold before our eyes. With the anger beside us as our friend, we have the energy to assertively address the issue. That emotional energy helps us stand up for the issue, communicate why we are angry, and express how we would like things to improve. We find courage to stand on the side of justice so that people are treated fairly.

Excavate your suppressed anger

I know my anger is beneficial and a most effective response to help me understand and deal with what life throws at me. But, as I said in chapter 10, I hate getting angry and wish I could switch it off. But others are possessed by and addicted to their anger. The sense of power that anger gives them exhilarates them. This was Martin Luther's experience. He said, "When I am angry I can write, pray, and preach well, for then my whole temperament is quickened, my understanding sharpened, and all mundane vexations and temptations gone."

Some commend this stand. But it was this chronically angry man who, to involve others in his rage and hatred, wrote *On the Jews and Their Lies*, wherein he advocated, just like another chronically angry man, the extermination of the Jewish race:

> We are at fault in not slaying them
> —Martin Luther

> We shall regain our health only by eliminating the Jew
> —Adolf Hitler

Regardless of how we feel about our anger, to varying degrees we all carry around within us buried anger from our past. All suppressed or chronic anger is an unhealthy, toxic poison.

Suppose you have an ongoing, unresolved disagreement with your spouse. Any anger connected to that unresolved disagreement does not go away. It takes up residence in rooms in your heart and festers away as resentment. The passing of time does not diminish it. Quite the contrary, it grows stronger as it feeds on today's anger. Weighed down by resentment, you can then explode at the slightest trigger. And your suppressed anger can spread from room to room inside your heart like a contagious flu, morphing into shame, alienation, contempt, hatred, restlessness, loathing, and sarcasm.

That suppressed resentment seeps out. It hijacks and twists the emotions, moods, and thoughts we experience today. The more suppressed anger we have down inside rooms in our heart, the easier, faster, and more intensely our anger gets triggered today, and the less successful we will be at managing our anger positively. If ignored, our suppressed anger will cut us off from other emotions and create in us an angry temperament in an angry body. And if all this is not enough, our suppressed anger attacks our physical body and shortens life-spans. It distorts our core values. Martin Luther believed his murderous hatred of Jews was what God valued. And many of us are not even aware we carry lots of suppressed anger around in our bodies.

To excavate your suppressed anger, take time to exhaustively describe your history of anger, past and present. In *Honor Your Anger*, Beverly Engel says, "We can't change what we don't acknowledge." You can begin by looking at ways you have recently managed and expressed your anger. What worked? What did not? Where did your anger go? Focus on the intensity of your anger and all the thoughts that raced through your mind. Be brutally honest and as thorough as possible in describing your experiences with anger (chapter 4). Write down or tell your trusted companion everything, no matter how negative, frightful, shameful, or hateful. At every turn, avoid generalizations. Be specific, use names. Do not sanitize, edit, censor, or polish anything. Pay attention to other emotions. Carry your thoughts about your anger across the barrier of your skin and into the light (chapter 4). Explore what triggered your anger (chapter 5) and reflect on what good can come about (chapter 6).

Also, go on an archaeological expedition down into rooms in your heart and excavate suppressed anger, some of which can go back to childhood. You may have to re-enter rooms in your heart multiple times to get it all (or as much as possible). So long as your suppressed anger and resentment stay in the dark, they fester. The truth is always your friend even if getting at it is painful. Chances are, you will feel unbelievable resistance inside as you journal your history with anger. But when you confront and embrace the facts about your personal history, you will find the courage to change.

Beating yourself up with guilt and shame is not the purpose of journaling your history of anger. Keep in mind, if you feel guilty while confronting your history with anger, it is actually a good thing. It means you violated one of your core values and did something you wished you had not done. Despite the discomfort, how can seeing that be anything but a good thing?

Here are some questions to guide you:

1. Do you usually express your anger by directing it outward (for example, by yelling) or inward (for example, in severe self-criticism), or both?
2. What were the attitudes toward anger in your family growing up?
3. How was anger expressed in your family?
4. What commonly triggers your anger?
5. Have you expressed your anger as a way to control someone else or in a way that led someone to be afraid of you? What happened?
6. Describe how you have been angry at one person and taken it out on someone else.
7. Are yelling and other forms of violent, aggressive behavior ever acceptable and right to you?
8. Think of occasions when you expressed your anger inappropriately. How might you have expressed your anger differently?
9. If you are about to enter a situation that is likely to trigger your anger, what might you do to prepare yourself?
10. Describe what a healthy expression of anger looks like for you?

12

Shame and the Disintegration of the Self

IN CEBU IN THE heart of the Philippines, a young unmarried girl takes her baby to church to be baptized. But instead of being blessed and immersed in the love of Jesus, the pastor tells the girl she is a sinner and rebukes her for having sex with a boy, not her husband. The pastor shovels shame on her and tells her the child may well grow up to become just like her. He calls her out and in front of family and friends asks her if she feels ashamed for letting a boy do this to her. Let not the pastor's heart be troubled. For the shame that the ordained minister impregnated in her will gestate deep inside her and give birth to a paralyzing sense that she is unlovable, worthless, beyond repair, and, as Merle A. Fossum and Marilyn J. Mason say, "not fully valid as a human being."

Shame has its own catechism. Every day and until the girl draws her last breath, her shame will relentlessly and viciously tell her to hate herself. Her shame will remind her that love and acceptance are things she does not deserve. Bowed down with shame, her inner implosion will be effortless. That man merely reinforced in the recesses of her inner being what she already knew. She will never need reminding that she is a heap of shame fit only to be sent to hell because God loathes her and finds her disgusting.

And that shame will beget more shame as it gets passed down from mother to child. John Bradshaw says in *Healing the Shame That Binds You*, "One of the devastating aspects of toxic shame is that it is multigenerational." Children carry their parents' shame.

Kelly, a Canadian-born Chinese, grew up in the shadow of her older brother Henry. As kids, both learned piano but Henry was sent to advanced science camps and got to go overseas as an exchange student. Kelly drifted to dancing and drawing. When dad and mom had people over, the talk was all about Henry's brilliance and accomplishments, and how Henry was going to Harvard. Her parents even bragged about Henry's good looks. Kelly's name was rarely spoken. Listening from the shadows, Kelly felt shame, disappointment, and anger. Having learned from her parents how to yell, she raged back in ever-growing resentment, "It's easy to see how this is all going to play out. Your trophy son goes to Harvard, but you'd be happy if I married some rich Chinese guy and gave you grandsons!" Left alone in her inner darkness, her shame whispered to her to annihilate herself. That would get their attention, Kelly reasoned. But thanks to an insatiable curiosity and unquenchable hunger to learn, Kelly drove herself academically and in athletics. When she got admitted to a prestigious school, her worth in the eyes of her parents skyrocketed. Kelly finally got a coveted spot on her parents' trophy wall.

"Shame," Brené Brown says in *I Thought It Was Just Me (but it isn't)*, "is the intensely painful feeling or experience of believing we are flawed and therefore unworthy of acceptance and belonging." This shame is the first emotion mentioned in the Bible. Adam and Eve were naked and unashamed (Genesis 2). Prior to eating the forbidden Philippine mango—how can anyone resist Philippine mango?—transparency and integrated wholeness filled their relationships. But after eating, Adam and Eve were ashamed of being themselves. Terrified of belonging and estranged from each other and God, Adam and Eve straight away made clothes to hide from each other, from God, and from themselves. Weighed down by shame, they just wanted to hide.

We can see how shame works in attitudes toward childlessness. In ancient Jewish culture many people thought God blessed married couples by giving them children. And not to have a child meant you were not blessed by God, and worse, God had cursed you and was punishing you for some sin in your or your family's past. We might suppose Rachel was playing the drama queen when she whined at Jacob, "Give me children, or I shall die!" But in a culture where a girl's market value was measured by breeding capacity, we can conclude she was in despair (Genesis 30). Shame devastated a childless woman like Rachel. It takes no work of pulp fiction to imagine people evaluating her, "Repent of your sins and God will give you children!"

Today, shame rips apart women wanting children but not able to. Being around other people's children can be heartbreaking. If they go to church and hear on Mother's Day how God blesses people with children, they go away knowing God hates them, is punishing them, or does not think them fit to be mothers.

Shame as a vehicle of change

Many parents shame or use the threat of shame to incite compliance to expectations in their children. In *The New Dare to Discipline*, James Dobson tells his readers how he was raised by his mother because dad was a full-time minister and on the road most of the time, preoccupied, I suppose, with giving it all to God and little troubled with being a kind father. At the principal's office, stern lectures and getting spanked with the "infamous rubber hose" did nothing to curb his goofing off or motivate him to get school requirements completed. His mother incessantly and invasively scrutinized his every move at school. It was as though his mother was always present even when absent to limit his space for privacy. Spankings had no positive effect on James Dobson and so his mother told him one day:

> If the principal ever calls me about your behavior, I promise you that the next day I'm going to school with you. I'm going to walk two feet behind you all day. I will hold your hand in front of all your friends in the hall and at lunch, and I'm going to enter into all your conversations throughout the whole day. When you sit in your seat, I'm going to pull my chair alongside you, or I'll even climb into the seat with you. For one full day, I will not be away from your side.

James Dobson says his mother was "a master at trench warfare." He was not kidding. He knew her character. She would follow through on this threat to shame him publicly were she ever to get that "fatal phone call." Her threat "absolutely terrified" him. In his words, "No punishment would have been worse!" It worked. The threat to humiliate him publicly bequeathed a permanent traumatic memory to his mind, broke his will, and brought about obedience to his mother's expectations. James Dobson offers her example to his readers as "a better idea" worth imitating.

No question, parental shaming and threats of humiliation like this bring about forced submission, but it is a form of bullying. It crushes the inner life of children. It has devastated countless children and teens. But because shame works deep inside the bodies of children and teens, parents are usually unaware of the damage they cause their own children. And were parents to see it, some would be quick to shield themselves, "Good heavens. It was for her own good. Look where Kelly is now!"

Comparison is another weapon of shaming. Beverly Engel and Barbara L. Frederickson map what goes on when people compare. In *Healing Your Emotional Self*, Beverly Engel says, "Comparison is always oriented toward determining worth or value—that is, who is 'better.'" And in *Love 2.0*,

Barbara L. Frederickson says when you compare "you stratify your social world into haves and have-nots."

I have no idea whether Peter, James, John, and the other apostles felt stratified or their worth diminished by what Paul wrote in 1 Corinthians 15. But I am comfortable saying a rift valley of veiled resentment opened between them. Paul built a ladder of "who works harder." He evaluated how hard he worked and how hard they worked. He then sketched the comparison: judge my work and theirs and you will see I work harder than all of them. For sure, the comparison gets laundered by talk of all-sufficient grace. But on the ladder, Paul put himself on the higher rung and the other apostles under his feet. When a person compares people using people as the standard of comparison, it generates shame, and shame imports bitterness and resentment into the fractured relationship.

Thirteen-year-old Sophie comes out on the short end of her mom's comparisons, "Sophie, did you hear Megan got an A+ on her test?" Mom feels satisfied with herself because she thinks she is parenting. But mom's good intentions are writing on water. Sophie's mom may as well have said what no child, teen, and adult should ever hear, "Shame on you, Sophie! You should be ashamed of yourself for not getting an A+ too." When Sophie hears her mom's comparisons, she thinks to herself, "No matter what I do, I don't measure up; mom takes more pride in someone else." Shaming Sophie communicates to Sophie that she is somehow unacceptable, inferior, and unlovable. Sophie was raised in what Michael Lewis, in *Shame: The Exposed Self*, calls "a shame-producing environment." Room after room in Sophie's heart filled with shame from encountering her mother's shaming.

And to repeat, just because mom does not see in Sophie's heart the destructiveness that her shaming causes Sophie does not mean the damage is not there. Denying it does not make the darkness go away. In *The Role of Shame in Symptom Formation*, Donald L. Nathanson says, "It is difficult to imagine that adults would subject children to so much measurement and comparison if they understood the amount of pain so created in their offspring."

Nevertheless, and despite all this, the painful feelings of shame and the shame-filled thoughts that Sophie experienced growing up are natural and normal. For sure, there is nothing life-giving about these feelings and thoughts. But they are not unusual or out-of-line. In fact, were Sophie not awash with shame as a result of her mom humiliating her, Sophie would be in grave danger. She could become unfeeling, shameless, incapable of empathy. And according to Paul Ekman and Mark G. Frank in *Lying and Deception in Everyday Life*, that is something all sociopaths or psychopaths share.

Is there then a place for constructive comparison? Absolutely. For children, the standard of comparison can be internal to the child. Let us return to Sophie and her mom and suppose Sophie's mom decides to stop shaming Sophie as a way to coerce obedience and bulldoze Sophie's will into submissiveness to parental expectations. Instead, she has her eyes only on her daughter. In love, she spends much time with her, listening to her, and she knows what Sophie is reasonably capable of achieving. She lays down her life in love for her daughter to help Sophie reach her full potential. "Sweetie," Sophie's mom says, "I love you and accept you the way you are. My love for you is not conditioned on how well you perform. I'm here for you and want to help you do your best." Having her mom believe in her may make Sophie reach for the stars.

Some years ago, my eyes were opened to how much trauma shaming inflicts. I'm sensitive now to when I am tempted to shame others. No matter how innocent I think my intentions might be, there is never a place for shaming or threatening to humiliate anyone. Having this awareness of and sensitivity to shame, I stopped using shame to motivate change in others.

The wisdom in shame that anticipates shame

Amnon is a sexual predator, someone who cultivates relationships solely for the purpose of sex. He is Tamar's stepbrother: different mom, same dad. Ever the user, Amnon wants Tamar's body to gratify his own megalomaniac lusts, and so he seizes Tamar to make his intentions known. By trying to reason with Amnon, Tamar is able, at least momentarily, to delay his predatory violence. Tamar proposes marriage, even though the Mosaic law prohibits marriage between them. It seems Tamar knew enough about dear dad's character to think he would put Amnon ahead of whatever Moses said (Leviticus 18; 2 Samuel 13).

Leaving aside why Tamar would ever propose marriage to Amnon, except perhaps she saw herself having to navigate between Scylla and Charybdis, she appeals to the scumbag by anticipating the shame she will carry if he incestuously rapes her. In other words, "Amnon, if you care for me, think of me and the situation you'll put me in!" And Tamar has integrity and empathy of character to think of Amnon and the sleazebag reputation he will get if he rapes her.

At this place in the story, Tamar has experienced shame that anticipates future shame. Both feel the same. Her sensitivity to this anticipated shame encourages her to do what is right, to stop the rape before it occurs. Tamar thinks that if she is raped, the rape will define her. This shame that anticipates future shame acts in a healthy, loving manner as Tamar's wise friend. It speaks to protect her.

Amnon, however, does not listen; he shamelessly and viciously rapes Tamar. And immediately after his predatory violence, his narcissistic lust morphs into disgust and loathing for wounded Tamar. The Roman historian Tacitus said, "It is a principle of human nature to hate those whom you have injured." Tacitus could have footnoted Amnon.

We do not glimpse Tamar's emotions after the rape but her behavior signals that her once gorgeous heart was now filled with shame. Although her feelings of shame are natural and normal, her shame—like intense anger—clouds her thinking. Tamar tells Amnon, "Send me away and that will be worse than you raping me!" Seriously? Either her thoughts were clouded or Tamar inhabited a world as bizarre as the one where Malibu Barbie acts as a mentor for young girls. Sweet Tamar was, to put it Christianly, screwed for life as a result of King David's son raping her.

This is what we are left with. Before the rape, Tamar's shame that anticipates future shame was her friend. It served a benevolent purpose to guide and shield her. Tamar heeded its discernment. But after the violent rape, the shame that Tamar endured can be compared to the pain and injury a Siberian Husky puppy would suffer after stepping into a hunter's trap.

Shame that anticipates future shame can also serve you well. Aaron Ben-Ze'ev says this shame can act as a built-in obstacle to immoral behavior. But only so long as you do not drive around the obstacle. Suppose you are contemplating some action that would cause you shame were your behavior to be publicly exposed. Listen to your wise friend: heed your feelings of shame that anticipate future shame, come to a full stop, and reconsider which way you want to go. Do not forget, if you continually ignore this friend, eventually your friend's voice will no longer be heard. That is what it means to be shameless.

The daily experience of the emotion of shame

You can feel shame when someone threatens you with rejection, compares you with someone else, puts you down, humiliates you in public, or makes a critical or disparaging comment about your body, clothes, education, ethnicity, family, gender, religion, or how you raise your kids. You can feel shame when your spouse ignores you after you decide to be vulnerable and express how you feel emotionally. If you have been brainwashed into thinking that being needy is a character flaw (more in chapter 18), you will feel shame when you want a hug from another mortal. You can feel shame when you do something embarrassing, when you fail at some task, or do not get enough likes on social media. What activates feelings of shame in one person may have no effect on someone else. The list of what triggers shame seems endless. And even if no one else shames you, you feel shame for just being a normal, flawed, less-than-perfect human being who does not always measure up to the person you want to be. Take chapter 3 to heart and learn to give yourself permission to just be enough.

Like our other emotions, we can take hold of our feelings of shame (chapter 4) and go digging for what Brené Brown calls our shame triggers. I mentioned above that shame can cloud and twist our thinking. Shame does so by getting us to believe that the shame trigger is actually the content of the thoughts of self-loathing, self-hatred, and self-disgust that pass through our minds when we feel shame. But the shame trigger is to be found elsewhere.

When we uncover our shame triggers, we are exposing areas in our life where we are insecure. When I first started teaching, I felt ashamed—embarrassed is the better word—when a student asked me a question for which I did not know the answer. My feelings of shame were exposing an area where I was insecure. I guess I felt I had to know all the answers. This goes to show that our sense of shame is not always a reliable guide. Thankfully I grew in self-confidence and do not ever feel ashamed when a student asks me a question for which I do not have the answer.

Let us revisit the story where David was relaxing in a cave and Saul entered (1 Samuel 24). Like a stealthy cat, David sneaks up and cuts off the corner of the king's cloak, a rather playful and harmless thing to do. David is then stricken to the heart for cutting off the corner of Saul's cloak. Again, we are not told the emotion David experienced, but I imagine he felt shame as his inner voice beat him up and filled him with self-disgust. It was also an emotional overreaction, marinated with hypocrisy. For had David wanted to take seriously that Saul was the Lord's anointed, he would have abandoned life as an outlaw man and submitted to this divinely-appointed authority.

Stricken to the heart, David is at a fork in the road. As an ingredient in vigorous self-leadership and as a means to manage his shame, David can speak truth to his uncomfortable feelings of shame and the accompanying thoughts of self-reproach. "Lighten up," he can tell himself, "It was just a fun prank." Speaking truth to his shame, the uncomfortable feeling would eventually evaporate, no harm done. But David does not speak truth to his shame. Instead, he beats himself up ruthlessly with his inner voice, and then—like the schoolyard bully he was—turns on his men and beats them up violently with his outside voice.

It is a life-long process taking the necessary time to explore what triggers your shame and how those triggers may shed light on areas of insecurity and vulnerability in your life. With your insecurities and vulnerabilities more and more in the light, you can decide whether you need to push through an area of vulnerability and grow, or make peace with that vulnerability, since you might not like the person you will become without that vulnerability. As a way to navigate our capacity for self-deception, I recommend sharing what you are thinking with someone who loves you. And sometimes when you feel you are being swept away by a tsunami of shame, you just have to ride out the storm. It will pass. Go to a movie or the gym to escape from yourself for a couple hours.

Shame hijacks guilt

As we saw in chapter 5, if you have truth as a core value, you will feel guilty when you to lie to someone. After all, you have slapped your core value in the face and it is not happy. Guilt serves up constructive criticism for encouraging positive change in behavior; you never want to harden your heart against guilt. But in a second, shame can effortlessly hijack the healthy guilt-response and pervert it into shame. And so, instead of thinking, "I did something bad when I lied," you rain down global condemnation on your head: "I'm a bad person."

A story about Moses' sister Miriam shows how shame takes guilt hostage (Numbers 12). Aaron and Miriam criticize Moses when he marries a dark-skinned girl from a land south of Egypt. The biblical writer thinks God sides with Moses, gets angry with Miriam, and punishes her with leprosy. According to the writer, Miriam transgressed. Guilt is a natural, healthy emotional response when we violate one of our core values (chapter 5). Guilt can motivate us to see and acknowledge error, and then make constructive changes to outlook and behavior. But as the biblical narrative continues, we see shame at work. The writer says, "If her father had but spit in her face, would she not bear her shame for seven days?" (Numbers 12:14, NRSV) The writer jumps from Miriam's transgression and corresponding guilt to Miriam contaminated with shame, a bad person, someone to be rejected and separated from. And that is what happens: "Miriam was shut up outside the camp for seven days" (Numbers 12:15, NRSV). This story visualizes what Lewis B. Smedes in *Shame & Grace* calls the "the shame equation": "One wrong act equals one bad person."

Years of bad habit and the fact that shame can feel like guilt work against us. When we violate a core value or make a mistake, way too often we label the uncomfortable feeling shame when we should identify it as guilt. The difference between shame and guilt often lies in how we understand the feeling. I said above we can speak truth to our emotions. When we feel ashamed and our thoughts are beating us up as a result of doing something, we can ask ourselves, should I describe how I feel as guilt or shame? It is never constructive to let our shame take hostage a healthy guilt-response. Brené Brown is not sticking a fork in your eye when she says, "Recognizing we've *made a mistake* is far different than believing we *are a mistake*." You did a bad thing and that makes you guilty; it never means you are a bad person.

Why is this important? When we appraise the constructive guilt-response as shame, we usually end up hiding from it. Unlike the guilt-response, our shame has zero interest in helping us see the truth, discover our shame triggers, and change behavior. Quite the opposite, our shame wants to keep kicking us in the head until we lay facedown in the dirt, immobile and paralyzed. And there is more. Again, to draw from Brené Brown, "The danger of telling ourselves that we are bad, a cheat, and no good, is that we eventually start to believe it and own it."

13

The Humiliated Fury of Buried Shame

MICHAEL LEWIS, IN *SHAME: The Exposed Self*, speaks of buried shame's elusive, "chameleon nature." He says, "Shame is like a subatomic particle. One's knowledge of shame is often limited to the trace it leaves." Our buried shame hides behind distorted emotions, clouded memories, twisted motivations, and inaccurate thinking. Our buried shame annihilates life and light and love. Brené Brown says in *I Thought It Was Just Me (but it isn't)*, "The less we understand shame and how it affects our feelings, thoughts and behaviors, the more power it exerts over our lives."

A hideous, vile enemy is one hundred percent of the buried shame we carry in our bodies, sometimes from the cradle to the grave. From its encampment deep inside us, our buried shame wages a war of carnage and destruction across the tapestry of our lives. It does this even when we are not aware it is there, which is usually the case. Our buried shame insidiously sculpts our day-to-day feelings. Buried shame gives birth to some of the shame we feel today, and today's shame begets more buried shame. Shame seeps down into the cracks and crevices of our inner lives. It shapes our thoughts and feelings about ourselves, our sense of worth, and how much we like ourselves. "In this way," John Bradshaw says in *Healing the Shame That Binds You*, "shame becomes basic to one's sense of identity. One becomes a shame-based person."

Buried shame leaves us with an empty void inside. Parker Palmer speaks of this empty void in *A Hidden Wholeness*, "I have met too many people who suffer from an empty self. They have a bottomless pit where their identity should be—an inner void to fill with competitive success, consumerism, sexism, racism, or anything that might give them the illusion of being better than others."

Our buried shame drives so much behavior

Buried shame drags us along paths to anti-social behavior, self-abuse, abuse of others, and addiction. In *Facing Shame*, Merle A. Fossum and Marilyn J. Mason say, "Addiction and shame are inseparable." Buried shame encourages some people to rarely express themselves, others to babble incessantly. Both can be strategies for people who want to hide. Our inner lives, now shame-based, become a shame-producing environment that drives how we interact with ourselves and others. Helen Block Lewis, who gave us "humiliated fury," says in *The Role of Shame in Symptom Formation*, "Shame is ubiquitous."

We would not give voice to our buried shame in the ways we do unless strategies like addiction were in some limited measure effective. We exert much energy to disconnect ourselves from the pain of our shame. But the rupture and disintegration of the self is the price we pay for leaning on these coping mechanisms.

How we deal with our buried shame varies from person to person. We have already witnessed one typical way. We pass it on. We shame our children (Sophie's mother; James Dobson's mother), those under our leadership (King David), or a churchgoer (the pastor in the Philippines). In *Shame: The Power of Caring*, Gershen Kaufman says, "By defeating and humiliating the victim, the perpetrator momentarily becomes freed of shame."

People pleasing is another common way to cope. Of course, pleasing others is not bad but not at the cost of surrendering adherence to core values, unique individuality, and full self-responsibility. To outrun the pain of shame, a son who has grown up in a shaming environment may live to please the father who shamed him. The son will probably consider it love. And the father, driven by twisted motivations, may himself be dependent upon, even addicted to, his son's adoration: emotional poison to numb his own shame and obstruct his son's maturation.

The Apostle Paul had been a people pleaser. Looking back, he wrote: "If I were still pleasing people, I would not be a slave of Christ" (Galatians 1:10). With that word "still," Paul admitted, "I used to be a people pleaser but not now." People pleasers tend to fret too much about what others think of them. They violate core values, throw integrity to the wind, and permit others to abuse them, use them, or walk over them.

People pleasing becomes unfair to family relationships when family members embrace traditions that dictate children must submit to parental expectations for them into adulthood. And some read "into adulthood" into the Bible's honor your father and mother (Exodus 20:12; Ephesians 6:2). Three questions: (1) Do you think that when a daughter or son carries this idea into marriage, that she or he is giving to a parent the loyalty and faithfulness that their spouse desires and deserves? (2) Why do you think some parents preserve the parent-child relationship "into adulthood" and not give the relationship freedom to evolve into an adult-adult relationship? (3) Does requiring children to submit to parental expectations "into adulthood" open the door to parents abusing power in the family?

Another way people deal with their shame is the opposite of people pleasing. People dish out emotional, physical, or verbal aggression against those who shamed them, or against anyone nearby. Shame does not discriminate. It chokes relationship-enhancing expressions of anger and turns it into a consuming flame. Anger and rage can insulate a person, including children, against the painful, destabilizing feelings of shame. Parents who raise a child in a shaming environment need not be surprised when their child turns to hitting other kids on the playground, tormenting the pet cat, or destroying toys. Most violent behavior is learned and not kids just being kids. Underneath much violent behavior in children and youth is buried shame.

Driven by the pain of buried shame, others shed their own blood, literally and figuratively. Self-abuse manifests itself, for example, in cutting oneself, engaging in dangerous and risky behavior, compulsive sexual conduct, addictions, and suicide. As a strategy "to relieve unbearable emotional pain," Judith Lewis Herman says in *Trauma and Recovery*, "physical pain is much preferable to the emotional pain that it replaces." Violence against oneself is, she says, "a form of self-preservation." Self-slaughter is where buried shame, from the trauma of abuse and hopelessness of despair, takes many thousands of girls and women in China every week who kill themselves.

Lots of shame-laden people become narcissistic. In *Shame: The Exposed Self*, Michael Lewis calls narcissism "the ultimate attempt to avoid shame." I have said enough about narcissistic people in chapter 7. Countless others fade away inside. Overwhelmed by buried shame, they let go of dreams of education, career, bettering themselves, and becoming the person they want to be. To borrow from "Love Me," a Katy Perry song about shame, their insecurities always seem to get the best of them. They withdraw from genuine love and run from deeper friendships. The fears and risks of transparency, vulnerability, and possible rejection are just too great. Working behind the scenes in their inner darkness, buried shame silently gnaws away at their sense of self-worth, self-confidence, and their capacity to love themselves and others. Buried shame gets in the way of love.

Addiction to power keeps insecurities on a short leash and insulates from the shame tucked away in one's inner darkness. In *Money, Sex & Power*, Richard J. Foster says, "Power is often called 'the best aphrodisiac.'" Richard Nixon had said power is the ultimate aphrodisiac. Leaders who must have power work their way up the hierarchy and then place themselves above meaningful accountability. If you criticize their idea, they will take it as a personal threat. They will not forget. They have a ravenous need to be honored and feel powerful, both of which are satisfied when they abuse power and dishonor others.

These power addicts ignore due process and arbitrarily and abusively fire someone below them, so they can get off on power and assert their authority. They will spread malicious lies about you and then preach a sermon on truth. Power addicts always find followers willing to extend loyalty and obedience to them. The followers want to wield the same power some day. In the home, a father and husband who lusts for power will expect submission from wife and children and, if Christian, will use the Bible to enforce submission from his family. So long as he gets his way, he will be Prince Charming. But hell hath no fury like a control-freak who does not get his way.

We can add perfectionism (not the same as pursuing excellence). The compulsion to be perfect, a form of self-abuse, allows no room to be human. Perfectionism inevitably fails (chapter 3). By striving for the impossible, a chasm opens between the perfection we are supposed to be and the imperfect we are and always will be. This gap relentlessly triggers feelings and thoughts of anxiety, bitterness, discouragement, failure, guilt, inertia, joylessness, self-hatred, stress, and more shame.

Gershen Kaufman says in *Shame: The Power of Caring*, "A perfectionist never has developed an *internal* sense of how much is good enough." Chapter 3 was about accepting ourselves as frail, likeable, normal, flawed, far-less-than-perfect human beings, who are profoundly deserving of love and capable of giving love. But I can read chapter 3 every day to fight perfectionism and buried shame, and it will never be enough. I must intentionally walk a path of emotional health and learn how to own, recognize, and trust my emotions. I have to listen to and express my emotions in healthy, relationship-enhancing ways (chapters 4–6).

When we exercise this self-leadership and self-responsibility, we become more accepting of ourselves and no longer afraid to be ourselves. We give ourselves permission to just be enough. We no longer pretend we can or ought to walk on water. Yes, Matthew 5.48 said, "Be perfect," but the context of Jesus' teaching helps me understand what he meant, "Excel at love." That can be done with feet of clay.

Excavating and exposing buried shame

The good news is, there is a path forward. We can learn to manage our shame with greater effectiveness, build resilience to keep our heads above water, and to varying degrees, reduce buried shame. But "the bad news is," Brené Brown says, "there's no way to permanently rid ourselves of shame."

As easy as the path is to understand, the way forward is intensely pain-filled and difficult. Some people would prefer to have all their teeth extracted without anesthetic than deal with buried shame. For our buried "toxic shame," John Bradshaw says, "masks our deepest secrets about ourselves." That is one reason why the inner journey of excavating and exposing buried shame can be so painful. I would add that sometimes those deep secrets are about others too. We want to keep these secrets—often truth we do not want to face—in the darkness.

If there is another reason why the inner journey of excavating and exposing buried shame is so painful, it is this: taking hold of our shame is like handling fire to fight a raging, cataclysmic fire. Shame seems to always burn.

I do not recommend going after your buried shame alone and especially so if you have experienced abuse in the past or wonder if you have (chapters 15–16). But shame wins when you are silent about it. Buried shame loses its grip on you when you drag it into the light and talk about it. That means going down into rooms in your heart and bringing the shame out, not just into your thoughts, but across the barrier of your skin where you tell someone about it or write about it. Brené Brown says, "Owning our story can be hard but not nearly as difficult as spending our lives running from it. Embracing our vulnerabilities is risky but not nearly as dangerous as giving up on love and belonging and joy—the experiences that make us the most vulnerable. Only when we are brave enough to explore the darkness will we discover the infinite power of our light."

I enormously enjoyed the 2015 Disney movie *Cinderella*. The first time Cinderella (Lily James) and the Prince (Richard Madden) look into each other's eyes deep in the forest, he disguises his identity by introducing himself by his father's pet name for him, Kit, and by saying he is an apprentice to his father at the palace. For her part, Cinderella evades Kit's questions as to who she is. Kit believes she is a good honest country girl. The second time they meet, Kit is to select his bride. At the royal ball at the palace, Cinderella is enveloped in the love and magic of her fairy godmother's spell (Helena Bonham Carter) and discovers Kit is the Prince. He thinks she is a princess. Out of shame Cinderella continues to hide who she truly is.

Her home is where they meet the third time. The Prince, now his Majesty, has been looking for the owner of the glass shoe. Cinderella finds courage to show herself without disguises. As Cinderella makes her way down the stairs, her fairy godmother narrates these words, "Would who she was, who she really was, be enough? There was no magic to help her this time. This is perhaps the greatest risk that any of us will take: to be seen, as we truly are."

In excavating and exposing our buried shame and all the painful memories down there in rooms in our heart, we learn to tell our own story. Somewhere along the way we come to see and accept that we are enough.

14

Sadness

Nights Long and Filled with Misery

IN HER *THE EMOTIONALLY Healthy Woman*, Geri Scazzero relates how she grew up being told sadness was unacceptable for Christians. And in *I Thought It Was Just Me (but it isn't)*, Brené Brown tells the story of a woman who lost her daughter to cancer. The woman's minister told her it was selfish of her to grieve as her daughter was with God. She hated the pastor and God for their heartless cruelty. It took her years to get over the trauma of humiliation and permit herself to grieve.

Where did Geri Scazzero and that minister get the notion it was wrong to feel sadness? As we will see below, not from Jesus. Revelation 21:4 may be one place. That author concocted the idea that sorrow, crying, and pain would not exist in eternity. So why be sad today? The Apostle Paul may be another. He said, "We don't want you to be in the dark, brothers and sisters, concerning those who have fallen asleep, lest you grieve as those who have no hope" (1 Thessalonians 4:13).

Jesus journeyed with sadness. When he heard John the Baptist had been murdered, he withdrew to a lonely place to grieve (Matthew 14). Lazarus, Martha, and Mary were also dear to Jesus. Lazarus died and had been dead four days when Jesus arrived at their home. He saw Mary's tears and was "deeply moved in his inner being and in turmoil inside himself" (John 11:33). Scoured by grief, he wept. Jesus held out hope of resurrection to Martha but still cried buckets. Jesus' love and deep emotional connection for his friends took him there (John 11).

In Gethsemane Jesus emptied his heart out to God with noisy sobbing and wailing. Jesus was then arrested and taken away, with Peter trailing at a distance. Later, after Peter disowned Jesus, Jesus turned and looked at him

(Luke 22). Did Jesus look at Peter to shame him into self-loathing? Or did Jesus look at Peter to show he loved him and would be there beside him in his bitter sadness? The passage offers no clues, but I think it was love in the heart of the Man of Sorrows. Someone at home with his own grief does not demean others by telling them it is selfish, sinful, or unspiritual to grieve. Jesus' life illustrates what he meant when he said, "Blessed are those who mourn" (Matthew 5:4).

Let's return to Paul. Did he teach that believers should strive to be emotion-free like the Stoics and some eastern religions? The Stoics taught that emotions are not reliable guides and that when we understand the truth about death—a matter of indifference—we will be free from grieving. Did Paul reach the same conclusion if for different reasons? Why mourn the loss of loved ones if they are in heaven and will participate in the resurrection? If Paul taught this, he did not get it from Jesus. There is, I think, another way to look at what Paul said.

When we step back and understand Paul's teaching against the contours of his life, we see he was no stoic. Prior to writing 1 Thessalonians, Paul believed Christ was going to return in his lifetime and probably taught this at Thessalonica. Some believers eventually died. This rattled the Thessalonian believers since Paul had taught everyone was going to be taken up to heaven at the imminent Second Coming. 1 Thessalonians 4:13–18 is Paul's response. He says those who died are not kicked off the bus because they died. He says believers should see the death of their loved ones through the lens of the resurrection. Grief with hope, yes; grief without hope, no. That is what I think 1 Thessalonians 4:13–18 says.

Then there are those places across his letters where Paul expressed sadness and grief. He spoke of the "great anguish and unceasing grief" he had for his people (Romans 9:1–3). His sadness connected his inner world with the world outside him, and his grief helped him make sense of it. Paul did not think feeling sad was contrary to faith or harmful to his spiritual well-being. Paul drew close to people and was emotionally invested. Paul knew love means shedding a tear or two. And there was that incident in Asia I spoke of in chapter 7. Something so oppressive brought Paul to a place where he was unbearably overcome and despaired of life.

Alfred Alvarez, in *The Savage God: A Study of Suicide*, mentions a Robert Lowell who "once remarked that if there were some little switch in the arm which one could press in order to die immediately and without pain, then everyone would sooner or later commit suicide." I cannot see Paul pressing that switch. But devoured by depression, I can see him putting himself in harm's way and be martyred. Suicide disguised as martyrdom; more common than we think.

Substitute "martyrdom" for "suicide," and Paul Ekman could have footnoted Paul when he said in *Emotions Revealed*, "Despair can overwhelm even the will to live, motivating a suicide. Emotions triumph over the will to live." Paul never judged himself as lacking faith or having sinned when he endured joyless despair and black depression. Rather, he saw his pain as an opportunity for growth. Paul's experiences with sadness and depression make no sense if he taught grief and sadness are not welcome emotions.

Riley needs you

In the Disney-Pixar movie, *Inside Out*, twelve-year-old Riley (voiced by Kaitlyn Dias) moves from Minnesota to San Francisco. Riley's emotion Joy (Amy Poehler) feels Riley can adjust to her new life with only her help. Maybe some help from Disgust (Mindy Kaling) to deal with broccoli pizza, but no need for anger, fear, and sadness. At one point, Joy takes a stick of chalk, draws a circle on the floor, calls it the "circle of sadness," and tells Riley's emotion Sadness (Phyllis Smith) that her job is to make sure sadness stays inside the circle. But later, Joy learns that Riley's imaginary friend Bing Bong (Richard Kind) needs Sadness. Riley was growing up and no longer needed her imaginary friend. Bing Bong was suffering sadness for the loss of a friend. Joy connects the storyboards and sees that, like Bing Bong, Riley needs Sadness too. If Riley is going to hold on to memories of her past in healthy ways and adjust to her new life, she needs to feel Sadness over what she lost when she moved.

We saw in chapter 11 how anger and love can team-up so we can address what needs our attention. *Inside Out* shows us how joy and sadness can also be friends who work well together to help us. I live this *Inside Out* truth. I can choke my sadness to death, but killing it destroys my love for another person. I will not run away from my sadness, although the weight of my sadness is not always easy to shoulder. At the core of what it means for me to be me, the firm root of joy flourishes (more in chapter 17). It anchors and saturates my sadness. I will make it through because of the friendship of joy and sadness in my life. This is where my love makes me stand.

Nehemiah and sadness of heart

How might things have played out had Nehemiah not embraced sadness? When his brother Hanani came back from Jerusalem and told him how bad things were, Nehemiah was crushed due to a deep emotional attachment to Jerusalem. But rather than treat his grief as an unreliable guide and matter of indifference, Nehemiah gave himself lots of space to be overwhelmed with sorrow.

Nehemiah was sensitive not to wear his emotions on his sleeve when he showed up for work at the court of Artaxerxes (ruled 465–424 BCE). But on this occasion his sadness leaked out. The King of Persia sensed Nehemiah's pain and, instead of ignoring it, asked about the sadness that showed on his face. Nehemiah became afraid. Did he sense what Daniel Goleman, Richard Boyatzis, and Annie McKee say in *Primal Leadership*, that interacting with one's boss leads to bad feelings like frustration, disappointment, and sadness "about nine out of ten times"? There was nothing for Nehemiah to fret about. He had a boss who felt comfortable in the presence of other people's emotions. Nehemiah explained what was behind his sadness and the King of Persia asked how he could help.

Nehemiah's sincere sadness moved Artaxerxes compassionately. This story shows how, just like Riley in *Inside Out*, Nehemiah needed his sadness. His sadness was soaked with values about what was dear to him. Without this emotional investment, it is unlikely Nehemiah would have cared to do anything about Jerusalem (Nehemiah 1–2).

Job and depression

Once upon a time, *Ha-satan* returned from a walkabout on the earth. God and he met up, and God wondered if *Ha-satan* had checked in on Job during his travels. For God had measured Job against everyone and concluded there was no one more blameless, more devoted, and more afraid of him. Hearing this, *Ha-satan* pounced. Would Job still fear God if God added no value to his life? *Ha-satan* accused God of putting a fence around Job and pampering Job with prosperity.

The evil that Job dreaded now happened. The lives of his ten children were snuffed out. What a monumental and futile waste of time it turned out to be, Job thought to himself, interceding with God on their behalf, sanctifying them, rising up early in the morning to offer all those stupid sacrifices for them, and then God capriciously let slip the dogs of war. If this was not enough, his property was stolen or destroyed, and he was afflicted with grotesque sores over his body to such an extent his friends did not recognize him. He tore his clothes, shaved his head, fell to the ground, and worshiped, spotlighting God's responsibility and role, "The Lord gave, and the Lord has taken away; blessed be the name of the Lord" (Job 1:21, NRSV; Job 1:1–21; 2:10; 3:25; 42:11).

Hearing what happened, Eliphaz, Bildad, and Zophar comforted Job and provided stability for him as he treaded the well-trodden path out of darkness. They sat with Job in consoling silence for a week and spoke only after Job spoke. Their words echoed God's word from Deuteronomy and Psalms. Job's friends had learned that people prosper in this life in everything they do when they delight in righteousness and stay off paths sinners tread. They believed "there is a deep structure of justice at the heart of existence" (Carol Newsom in *The Book of Job*). Their friend just needed to wait patiently. The righteous always have "and they lived happily ever after" endings (Job 4:5–7; 42:10–17; Psalm 1; 5).

Job crashed into disillusionment, dissatisfaction, and despair. Gloom and deep despair washed over him. Major depression swallowed him. Job loathed his life and cursed the day of his birth. There was no joy in breathing anymore. Job thought what a fool he had been to think he could expect anything more from life or God than misery and sorrow. After all, "Human beings are born to trouble just as sparks fly upward" (Job 5:7, NRSV). His hopelessness and grief spawned irritability and frustration, anger and resentment. Bildad saw how anger was ripping Job apart (Job 5:6–7; 7:16; 9:21; 10:1; 14:1; 18:4).

In his depression Job lost so much weight his shriveled skin clung to his bones. Some people were judging Job's physical appearance as proof of sin. And his bed offered no rest. We witness in Job what Andrew Solomon says in *The Noonday Demon*, "Even though depressed people seek the oblivion of sleep, it is *in* sleep that the depression is maintained and intensified." Nights were long and filled with misery. Job thought God was terrorizing him with nightmares (Job 3:20–26; 16:8). In *Let Your Life Speak*, Parker Palmer says, "I understand why some depressed people kill themselves: they need the rest."

Others shamed Job, You called on God and lived a blameless life; look where it got you. Still others encouraged him to find comfort in God and God will set everything right. Job knew otherwise. Job's depression was exacerbated by lost confidence in a God whose character was supposed to make some sense, but instead God smashed Job's teeth (Job 6:4; 12:4; 34:6).

With the passing of days his friends came to interpret Job's life differently. If a rod of iron dashed Job to pieces, he must have deserved it. Fine, Job said, but all he asked was for God to show up and point out his transgression. Sin or no sin, Job knew God found him disgusting and was making his life sour. Job knew God had mercilessly torn him apart in his wrath even though he was innocent. Job knew God hated him and had come along and kicked him in the side of the head when he was already down (Job 7:11; 8:21; 10:1; 15:34; 16:7–11; 21:25; 27:2).

Job called God's moral goodness into question. How can God's behavior align with justice? Does God fly off the handle in rage and dish out miseries senselessly and for no reason? Would Job's suffering have been multiplied had he known what we readers know, that *Ha-satan* had pushed God's buttons and that God had actually destroyed him for no reason at all? Job suspected as much (Job 2:3; 9:17–18; 21:17–18).

Job railed against the tempest: You're a bully, a terrorist. I've lived my whole life terrified of the calamities you'd rain down on me if I didn't live a perfectly spotless life in righteousness. In dark depression, Job could not take enjoyment from anything that normally brought people pleasure. But then he reasoned God would consider it idolatrous if he did. Job saw that righteousness is pointless in an imperfect human. Job added, "It profits one nothing to take delight in God" (Job 34:9, NRSV; 31:23; 35:2–3).

His lament dripped bitterness and sarcasm:

> If I'd so much as put trust in wealth, taken pleasure from success in business, if I had glanced at an attractive girl, ignored the complaint of one slave, or left a stranger stranded in the street, if I had enjoyed a sunset, then in your eyes I'm utterly reprehensible and deserving of punishment. You detect a fleck of sin in me and you treat me brutally. You even take pleasure from it. The slightest infraction and you think I'm false to you. What's wrong with working hard and enjoying its rewards? Look how I've lived and look where it got me (Job 31).

Job prayed, "Let me alone, that I may find a little comfort before I go, never to return, to the land of gloom and deep darkness, the land of gloom and chaos, where light is like darkness" (Job 10:20–22, NRSV). Job thirsted for death, the one place God was not. Only there, away from God, would he rest (Job 3:20; 7:16). Job's logic is compelling: God, human life is just a vapor, to begin with. Why do you have to come along and make our lives even more miserable? Just leave me alone.

I read somewhere how Americans love tragedies with happy endings. That is how the Book of Job ends, except for Job's disposable ten children. But they were replaceable (Job 42:13). Yes, Job was bought off and died old and full of days (Job 42:10, 17), but I cannot help but think he learned his lesson, to cultivate his garden, keep his mouth shut, and proceed no further with voluntary words to God (Job 40:3–5; 42:3–6). Like no other literary work, the Book of Job offers us a compelling portrait of depression and despair in a person of faith.

Women, sadness, and depression

There is to be a wedding (Psalm 45). A king, who already has a queen and a harem of beautiful young play-toys, is about to marry a princess from some foreign land. She is drop-dead gorgeous and maybe fourteen or fifteen years old. The poet knows she was dragged unwillingly from her grandparents, siblings, friends, favorite foods, places where she played, and from her parents who probably arranged it and negotiated a handsome payoff for themselves and their sons. I imagine loneliness, paralyzing emptiness, and despondency overthrew the girl. Did the girl think she was brought into the world to be sold as a sex toy and breeder of sex toys for the Royals? Ashamed of her calling, did she curse her breasts and contemplate self-annihilation? The writer attempts to console her by giving voice to his core values: The king's going to lust after your body. He's your master and you must kneel down. Nor can you just lay there. But don't fret, you'll get to like it. What's more, wealthy people are going to use you to get access to the king, so get ready to receive gifts. All this is pretty cool stuff the poet fantasizes. Lacking anything that could remotely resemble empathy, he is unable to touch her heart and see her through her eyes. I think the poet's pity left her even more scarred in her despair and alone.

In any country, culture, home, workplace, and religion where females are treated as inferior, subordinate, subservient, less significant, less valued, and less equal than males, where females have second-class status or judged as property or an accessory, where females suffer lower economic, marital, religious, political, and social opportunities than males, females are susceptible to more resentment, shame, sadness, fear, depression, and abuse. In whatever form this inequality takes, it diminishes human flourishing.

Managing and mismanaging sadness

Joshua Wolf Shenk, author of *Lincoln's Melancholy*, wrestled with the enigma of Abraham Lincoln's life. Abraham Lincoln was overwhelmed by pessimism, sadness, despair, self-doubt, thoughts of suicide, and occasionally, utter collapse his entire life. He acknowledged and accepted his depression as a fact of his life. He energetically sought to understand, explore, and dissect his depression, what caused it, and what he could do about it. He developed the core values of perseverance and forbearance to persist and persevere. As a way to grind away and keep breathing, he had coping mechanisms, which included telling stories and jokes, writing poetry, and reading the Book of Job and Shakespeare's tragedies.

Abraham Lincoln sought good works outside himself that gave his life meaning, the most important of which was the vital cause of abolishing the everlasting wickedness of slavery. Abraham Lincoln ransomed his depression and it gave him clarity, discipline, and hope. He integrated his depression into his life and it fueled his mission as a leader. But never he got better. So let me ask, do you think Abraham Lincoln was happy?

We saw how Nehemiah gave himself plenty of time to feel grief and let it have its day. He neither hurried the grieving process nor did he hold on to it forever. It is not that the pain would have vanished entirely, but Nehemiah managed his sadness well and came to a place where he could stand on his feet, look forward, and shoulder responsibility.

But as we saw in chapter 4 we can mismanage sadness. A common way is to suppress sadness by means of anger. This does not mean, of course, that every time sadness and anger show up together, that anger is trying to crack down on sadness. Recall Job. Nevertheless, every book written on anger is a book about sadness. If sadness can deflate us and make us feel fragile and vulnerable, anger can invigorate us and give us a sense of control and power. If sadness makes us feel exposed, anger covers us with armor. No wonder we harness anger to (mis)manage sadness. Anger is bossy. It effortlessly pushes sadness down. But Beverly Engel speaks of the price we pay for using anger to numb sadness, "If you continually cover your sadness with anger, you risk seriously affecting your ability to experience true intimacy with others." Underneath much chronic anger is buried sadness.

Others take hold of their sorrow and never let it go. Maybe they feel that if they let it go, they will stop loving the person they lost. Or perhaps they do not let go so they can reek revenge on a person who hurt them: you messed up my life and I'm going to keep on suffering, just so you know how much you hurt me.

Unfortunately, the longer a person holds sadness, the more enslaved to it they become, and the harder it is to let go. Imagine holding a baseball loosely in your right hand. Your left hand can effortlessly snatch it away. But squeeze that baseball as tightly as you can and your left hand will not pry it out. Imagine the baseball is sadness. The longer you hold on, the tighter your grip becomes and—here's where the metaphor breaks down—the tighter the grip sadness has on you. So many wasted tears result. Remember what I said in chapter 5. Time is against us when it comes to dealing with buried emotions like sadness.

Sadness the teacher

Our sadness often helps us see things we need to see. Nehemiah's sadness told him just how deeply he cared and it got him (and the king) thinking about what he could do. For sure, sadness occasionally clouds thinking. But, like other emotions, sadness normally has something to tell us about how significant someone or something is to us. Where there is a problem, it is usually not with the emotion. It is that we do not want to hear the message. Recall how Alysha suppressed her sadness and disappointment about what was wrong in her relationship with Robert. Or recall how Alice Miller and Selena invented webs of lies so they did not have to confront the painful message their sadness was trying to tell them. Neither had mothers who loved them (chapters 1, 4–5).

To be sure, if there is something that needs doing we can courageously do it even though our sadness will not be the emotion energizing us to do it. But once our sadness has had its say, it will not be discouraging us to quit before we start, and it will not trip us up as we go.

When Geri Scazzero started to embrace her emotions, she saw that sadness, discouragement, and depression can be "teachers sent from God." She describes what happened when she stopped running from her sadness: "They formed passageways that led me into hidden truths about myself and God, and I have become a much more avid student of these emotions as result." Geri Scazzero came to a place where she could identify "with a common brokenness shared by all people on the earth." This enabled her "to be more compassionate towards the sadness of others." She says, "I am now convinced this is one of the greatest gifts I have to offer." Think about it. Had Nehemiah and Geri Scazzero not trusted and listened to their sadness or felt they did not need sorrow, they may have missed their vocational callings.

15

The Hideous Chamber of Horrors Called Abuse

IF I HAD A nickel for every time I have said to someone, don't underestimate the effects of abuse, I would—to quote Katy Perry—own the bank.

In every culture for all recorded history, the extent of abuse has been so astronomical, so pervasive, so pandemic, of such magnitude. Statistics underestimate how widespread abuse is. Many deny they have been or are in an abusive relationship. Admitting this truth changes forever how they see themselves and the abuser. The global acceptance, denial, or tolerance of abuse efficiently mask its extent.

Take Lot, that "righteous man" (2 Peter 2:7). He warned his neighbors, "Do not act so wickedly," and then offered his two disposable teenage daughters to them with words, "Do to them as you please". (Genesis 19:8, NRSV).

Or take Sigmund Freud and what he discovered in respectable, upscale Paris and Vienna. He said, "Almost all of my women patients told me that they had been seduced by their father." How did he eventually respond? He plugged his ears. He said, "I was driven to recognize in the end that these reports were untrue and so came to understand that the hysterical symptoms are derived from phantasies and not from real occurrences." He said, "It was only later that I was able to recognize in the phantasy of being seduced by the father the expression of the typical Oedipus complex in women." Most everyone trusted him.

Every father and step-father who has sexually abused his daughter or step-daughter can thank Sigmund Freud. For most everyone will think the little bitch is lying; it's just a girl's fantasy! "It is only today," Dave Grossman says in *On Killing*, "over a century later, that we have begun to accept and address the magnitude of sexual abuse of children in our society."

Seldom, if ever, has an abused person experienced only one kind of abuse, whether it be emotional abuse, emotional neglect, emotional smothering, physical abuse, abuse of power, sexual abuse, spiritual abuse, exploitation, or verbal abuse. In this chapter, child abuse, the emotional neglect of children, and spiritual abuse have my attention. Please do not infer that other kinds of abuse are any less evil and vile.

Child abuse and the emotional neglect of children

For much of my adult life I did not think I was abused as a child; now I know I was and its repercussions have been consequential. My twin brother and I were born early. A few days later, Keith walked out of the hospital and rode his tricycle home. I spent six months in the hospital undergoing multiple surgeries. Although the infant's brain is not developed to form conscious memories, it vacuums up so much.

It was not abuse because I had to be in isolation, but I suffered the trauma of emotional neglect all the same. I did not receive physical contact and emotional connectedness vital for an infant's maturation during that critical period. In the absence of physical contact and emotional connectedness, many infants and children do not develop a healthy impulse to shield and protect themselves when they get older. I have long joked about it, but it is no joke: all my life I have been beyond horrible at looking out for my interests. I used to think this was the spiritual thing to do.

When I was seven, a teen boy up the street sexually abused me a number of times. At the time I had no words to describe what I felt, but now I know I experienced shame and self-disgust. What also troubled me at the time was how I let it happen. Was I vulnerable because I did not have that natural and healthy impulse to shield and protect myself?

During my childhood I was emotionally neglected. My father would go to Keith's music performances and coach his sports teams, not mine. I was not hugged or told I was loved. I remember my dad being there for others, not for me. On one occasion I went with my father to visit his friend on a farm. During a meal my father's friend cut into me about my eating habits, and my father did nothing to defuse the aggression or defend me. For the weekend's duration, my father hung out with his friend, leaving me to wander the farm and look on from a distance. There was also physical abuse. Although infrequent, it was impactful. In my dad's anger I was spanked and hit, and on one occasion, he threw me to the floor and kicked me several times.

Growing up, insecurities, low self-image, and lack of self-confidence were my constant companions. I was never afraid of my dad, but I carried truckloads of resentment. I felt unlovable and unwanted. I hungered for attention but was taken to church and taught to deny myself. I excelled. Growing up believing it was a sin to be needy, I suppressed my neediness, fears, resentment, sadness, and shame by trying to forget about myself.

These suppressed emotions leaked out. Most of the time I kept my (metaphorical) demons down in the basement, but there were days those memories and repressed emotions forced their way up the stairs. I was cruel to small animals, destroyed things, provoked fights with my brother, and bullied the new kid at school. I am thankful that by the age of eight I stopped expressing my buried emotions through aggressive behavior, except on the hockey rink. Instead, I turned it all inward against myself in self-hatred and self-disgust.

As a teen, on New Year's Eve I would look back at the year that had been and think how unhappy I had been. My fears and unnoticed shame constantly tripped me up. I had self-doubts about my competence. Until I got to my mid-twenties, I found it hard to take sustained initiative. Then I discovered how research can be a powerful addiction to anesthetize my inner pain. I became über self-disciplined and this addiction sustained me for the next twenty years and still does, on the occasional day.

Any former resentment toward my father is gone. I am modestly better at looking out for myself but will always struggle. All the furniture (memories) is still down there in rooms in my heart but I have brought life and light and love to every room in my heart. I am my own best friend. But there is still that occasional day. In her book with the same title, Babette Rothschild says, "The body remembers." Does it ever.

My story describes just a few of the myriad symptoms of childhood abuse. I have mentioned other self-destructive behaviors throughout the book and will mention more below. Scientists now understand how abuse alters the central nervous system of children. Anything the central nervous system touches can be affected by abuse: eyesight, hormones (for example, for sleep and sex), and memory are three. But it is common for people to be skeptical about how deeply abuse damages children. Kids bounce back, they say. But children do not have armor to absorb abuse without it doing irreparable, permanent harm. This is another reason I speak of mending, not healing (chapter 3).

Parents inflict most child abuse. Many parents do not think their behavior is abuse. And sadly, many cultures encourage children, teens, and adults to keep a lid on the painful emotions and memories of the abuse they suffered as children. They are told or tell themselves:

- Your parents were under a lot of stress to make a better life for you;

- Who are you to complain? They were doing their best;

- I order you to forget it; it doesn't matter now;

Where the Bible has a voice, abusive parents are shielded behind "Honor your father and mother." Children get a Bible-thumping: "It does not matter how your parents treated you, you have to honor them." Many cultures say the same. But no biblical teaching or cultural tradition should ever to be used to disguise childhood trauma for something it is not, shield parents from appropriate blame, or help an abused person evade their past.

"Many parents neglect their children because they are simply incapable of being good parents." That is Beverly Engel in *Healing Your Emotional Self*. She says some parents are so self-absorbed that children must meet the parents' needs for attention and admiration. In other homes, despite what they say, parents have priorities higher than their children. Some abused and neglected children grow up to do to their own kids what they had suffered.

Spiritual abuse

You are in the presence of spiritual abuse when a person uses Scripture, God, or their position of authority in a religious institution to bully, coerce, control, dominate, subjugate, or terrorize you, shame you, make you feel guilty, or make you feel inferior, as a way to bring about compliance.

Spiritual abuse is present when

- that priest in Cebu shamed the young mom in church (chapter 12);
- a pastor tells the elders, "I feel God is telling me we're to buy the property and erect a church building." How can the elders disagree with God;
- a priest instructs a woman, "God hates divorce and so God requires you to stay in the abusive marriage";
- you go to a pastor about a problem and go away having been made to feel you are the problem;
- a woman builds up the courage to go to her pastor to tell him about the ongoing abuse in her marriage and she is told to go home, submit to her husband, and keep her mouth shut since to speak up would shame her family, pastor, and church.

When pastors and church leaders battle with people to establish their dominance and authority, you are in the presence of spiritual abuse. They expect to be obeyed. After all, they believe God put them in the church (mosque, temple, synagogue) to lead and it is all about loyalty to them. Their lust for power is more insatiable than any sex drive. They force submission to their unreasonable and sometimes arbitrary decisions so that they know they have compliant sheep.

Spiritual abuse is present when leaders in religious institutions put their behavior, words, and decisions above questioning, criticism, scrutiny, and accountability, or when they say, "Don't touch the Lord's anointed," and think they are the Lord's anointed.

On occasion I am involved in a conversation with someone who is deciding whether to stay in a church where the pastor or leader is spiritually abusive. I tell them they need to take responsibility for their decisions. That means no "I wanted to leave but God wanted me to stay." I ask, by staying will you be where you can grow as a person? If they decide to leave, I advise, Do not pull-pin. It is a military metaphor. Pull-pin happens when you write a letter or make some accusations that are comparable to pulling the pin on a grenade and throwing the live grenade back over your shoulder as you walk out the door. Because it is the truth does not make pull-pin okay. If you stay, you have a voice; if you leave, leave silently.

Assigning appropriate blame and taking responsibility

A mother reminds her daughter, "If you weren't born, I wouldn't have to sacrifice my life to raise you. I'd be able to buy things and travel." Her daughter is overwhelmed by shame, resentment, and self-destructive tendencies. Her suppressed emotions cry out for a cause. The teen effortlessly reasons, Mothers love daughters but I'm not loved. There's something wrong with me; I'm to blame.

Many people think nothing is to be gained by assigning appropriate blame. But if the daughter does not assign appropriate blame, she will blame the wrong person, herself. Or, if she brings God into the equation, she will be blinded by self-deception: God is punishing her, or the abuse is part of God's sovereign plan for her life.

If an adult abused you when you were a child or teen, you share none of the blame, regardless of your behavior. You were vulnerable, incredibly so. There are no shades of grey. It is different in adult-adult abusive relationships where navigating appropriate blame may not be so black and white.

I said in chapter 6 that you can speak truth to your emotions and they will respond. In like manner, when you find yourself blaming yourself for the abuse you endured, speak truth to your thoughts and feelings, 10,000 times if necessary. It will take time for your emotions to realign, but they will. After all, your emotions want to be on your side.

Tell yourself who is to blame. Name their name. But never only ruminate about it in your head. As I said in chapter 4, the truth needs to cross the barrier of your skin. Write the truth of who is to blame in your journal and tell the truth to a safe person you trust. By telling someone, you are, as Judith Lewis Herman says in *Father-Daughter Incest*, serving notice that you will no longer accept the burden of responsibility for your abuser's behavior.

Assigning appropriate blame takes you part way. Having to carry the full weight of responsibility for mending your heart and changing your behavior takes you the rest of the way. Yes, it is not fair. They messed you up but you have to shoulder responsibility.

There will be so much weighing against you taking responsibility. There is the feeling of helplessness that hems you in, there is the shame, there is all the time not spent taking responsibility. Time is always against you when it comes to dealing with your past (chapter 5). The longer you wait the harder it gets. Then there are the mental gymnastics you perform to justify stagnation: You hurt me so bad I'm going to keep screwing up my life so you'll always be reminded how much you hurt me.

What can happen when you take full responsibility? You can begin an inner journey that will lead you to take hold of the excruciatingly painful memories of abuse and suppressed emotions that reside in rooms in your heart. Once your painful past has been woven onto the tapestry of your life, you will be able to move freely in and out of those rooms in your heart as your own best friend. As mentioned earlier, there will always be some residual suppressed emotion and all the memories of abuse, but your past will no longer dominate you or bother you as much. As mentioned in chapter 1, when life and light and love fill these rooms in your heart, you will be able to leverage your past in beautiful and life-transforming ways.

Prayer can play a constructive role in helping you courageously see the full truth of the abuse and walk the life-long path of mending. But it is irresponsible to believe your traumatic past can be prayed away. I wish there were, but there are no short-cuts or miracles when it comes to bringing life and light and love to those rooms in your heart that contain traumatic memories of abuse and suppressed emotions.

If you are now in an abusive relationship or marriage, taking responsibility can mean taking your fear, resentment, sadness, and shame seriously, and listening to what these emotions are telling you. You will find courage to take a first concrete step toward removing yourself from the abuser (chapters 4–6). In *Trauma and Recovery*, Judith Lewis Herman says, "People discover that they have a reservoir deeper than they thought, even though they come out of that fight exhausted or crying and shaking like a leaf."

And you will be able to see your situation more clearly. For when terrified, you don't think straight. Abusers know this. They use charm one minute and terror tactics the next to produce instability in you and twist your thinking. It is called gaslighting (named after the well-worth-watching 1944 movie). They want you isolated in a captivity of profound passivity where, as Judith Lewis Herman says in *Trauma and Recovery*, you have relinquished all initiative, autonomy, and struggle.

To sustain your numbing surrender to his tyranny, you might pervert the Bible by thinking "Wives, subject yourselves to your husbands" at Ephesians 5:22 means God wants you to remain in an abusive relationship. Many church-going, abusive husbands quote this Scripture to their wives. If you stay in an abusive relationship, I ask you not to believe God supports your decision.

Never go it alone

Alice Miller says in *Banished Knowledge* that the "process of deepening one's insights" into the abuse of one's past "is never fully terminated." Facing your abuse is a life-long journey, but part of this life-long journey is a shorter journey. This shorter journey brings you to a place where you can say you have thoroughly and exhaustively dealt with all the abuse from your past that you are presently aware of. And it seems to be inevitably the case that when you get to the end of this shorter journey, you want to tell someone your story.

For this shorter journey, never go it alone. You will need a therapist, pastor, or close friend, a 'heart doctor'—not a cardiologist—who knows their way around the human heart, someone who will take your side and not allow you to evade the truth, someone who will walk beside you on your long journey out of hell. And it is worth keeping a journal where you reconstruct your whole story of abuse, in depth and in exhaustive detail. And on your life-long journey, you can add to it as you learn more about your past abuse.

Forgiveness and reconciliation

From birth until a young adult, Beverly Engel suffered emotional neglect, emotional abuse, physical abuse, and verbal abuse from her mother: constant fault finding, punished unfairly, beatings, name-calling, belittling (you're stupid and ugly), malice, indifference, ignored for days, and negatively compared to others.

In a climate of constant danger and frozen watchfulness, Beverly Engel became hypervigilant (Judith Lewis Herman in *Trauma and Recovery*, "the first cardinal symptom of post-traumatic stress disorder"), always on the lookout for an impending, merciless attack. She would double and redouble her efforts to be a mommy-pleaser. Children crave a loving parent. But no matter what she did, she could not satisfy the unreasonable expectations. From the age of three she had to care for herself but inevitably made mistakes. She would spill milk when making her own breakfast and her mother's vicious rage and contempt would pour down on her. Looking back, Beverly Engel said, "My mother, very good at presenting herself to the public as a warm, charming woman, suddenly became an angry, bitter witch whenever I caused her any trouble at all." As we read in *The Jekyll and Hyde Syndrome*, she blamed herself, "After all, everyone loved my mother, so it must have been my fault that she changed into such a terrible person."

Growing up an emotional orphan, the abuse filled her with shame, rage, self-loathing, and eventually indifference. Beverly Engel believed she was an evil, dirty, unacceptable human being. She developed lots of narcissistic tendencies that she did not fully see in herself until she listed symptoms of narcissism for her superb book, *The Emotionally Abused Woman*. All this set her up to be abused and abuse others. As a child she was sexually abused by three men, one of whom, the husband of a friend of her mother's, forced her to give him oral sex over a period of six months when she was nine-years-old. Sexualized at such an inappropriately young age, she began acting out sexually with neighborhood children. In *Breaking the Cycle of Abuse*, Beverly Engel continues:

> But nothing that had been done to me or that I had done to others at that point in my life compared with what came next. It happened one day when I was babysitting for a one-year-old boy. I was twelve years old. As I was changing his diaper I felt overwhelmed with an intense impulse to suck his penis. I was filled with a tremendous desire to feel the power of doing to someone weaker than myself what had been done to me. Fortunately, this impulse was followed by an overwhelming feeling of shame and revulsion. I was horrified at what I was thinking of doing—so horrified that it stopped me in my tracks.

Taking her vulnerability seriously, she decided not to babysit young boys again. She had a front-row seat for witnessing how abuse gets passed on. And she found empathy for others who experience the same intense impulse "to do to others what was done to them." Later, she was able to put herself in her mom's place and empathize with her. She decided to try to resolve her relationship with her mom and learn her mom's story. Eventually she forgave.

There were terrifying risks. Her mom could have malevolently ripped into her daughter, telling her she was sick in the head for thinking such things. There was also the uncertainty whether her mom would open up about her own past. Had her mom not answered her questions, Beverly Engel would have been denied knowledge she needed to mend a huge rip in the tapestry of her life.

Should you keep hoping he will change?

At 1 Corinthians 13:7, Paul says love "hopes all things." Does this mean you should forever hope and hang on, believing that if you give him more chances, keep on excusing his behavior, put your needs aside and sacrifice more, submit more, pray more, that he will eventually respond to your sacrifice with love? But to sacrifice oneself is just a form of self-mutilation.

I recently had lunch with a friend whom I mentored. For twenty years, she had been in an emotionally, physically, and verbally abusive marriage. The beatings put her in the hospital on more than one occasion. She walked a path of change and her husband eventually stopped being abusive. But not before she saw her son grow up to become like his father. I said to her, "The fact that your husband changed is going to give women hope their abusive husbands can change." She knew what I meant. For I was speaking of the same kind of hope that Tadeusz Borowski, Auschwitz Extermination Camp inmate, described, "We were never taught to rid ourselves of hope, and that is why we are dying in the gas-chambers." Some hope is like swallowing sand.

There is only one right answer to the question, should you forever hope, and that is, no. Forgiving seventy times seven does not mean having to give 490 chances. Hope has limits. Henry Cloud and John Townsend call "defensive hope" this hope that never stops hoping. Defensive hope protects a person from taking seriously their sadness and pain. Defensive hope blinds a person from seeing the truth about the person abusing them, that despite all their empty promises, this is the way they are and most likely they are never going to change. After all, if he wants to change he will and not make promises. In *Safe People*, Henry Cloud and John Townsend say, "Humans are incredible optimists when it comes to destructive relationships. For some reason we think that a person who is hurtful, irresponsible, out of control, abusive, or dishonest is going to change if we just love them correctly or more or enough." They also say, "Defensive hope is one of the biggest reasons we allow destruction to continue in life."

Hope, on the side of life and light and love, points to the sun and is a ladder out of darkness. That other hope sets fire to the ladder and leads to delusion, destruction, and the inertia of despair.

16

On the Spanking and Beating of Children

THE BIBLICAL BOOK OF Proverbs encourages parents to beat their children with a rod since, as Proverbs 20:30 says, one way to reach the innermost parts of a child and *scour* away the wickedness there is by inflicting *beatings*, *blows*, and *bruises*. *Polish* the surface of a child's body with *contusions*, *lacerations*, *welts*, and *bleeding wounds*, and a *personality brilliantly polished* results. Commentaries on the Book of Proverbs provided the italicized words. Old Testament scholar, Tremper Longman, in his commentary, *Proverbs*, says that so long as a child is not "hurt seriously," the application of the "harsh" teaching of Proverbs 20:30 "helps transform the heart" of the child. For him, the teaching of Proverbs "calls into serious question whether modern child-rearing strategies are more beneficial than biblical wisdom."

The Book of Proverbs has provided building blocks for what is popularly called the Judeo-Christian concept of parenting. Christians are no more bound to follow the teaching on child discipline set forth in Proverbs than they are the Mosaic laws on Sabbath (Exodus 20) or circumcision (Genesis 17). Nevertheless, we can still ask, does the teaching in Proverbs about parents beating their children with a rod benefit a child's character formation?

The rod of Proverbs 10:13 is the tool for excavating the resident evil in a child's heart. Back then, no one interpreted the rod figuratively or metaphorically or thought it was a long wooden spoon suitable for stirring soup or smacking saucy children. The rod was used for tending livestock and beating slaves, and the Mosaic law recognized that slave owners occasionally beat their slaves to death. If a man did not have sword or spear, he showed up for battle with a rod. A poor man's weapon? Just the sight of a rod in a parent's hand would traumatize a child.

The Book of Proverbs serves up various arguments to motivate parents to beat their kids. Proverbs 13:24 makes it a matter of love: "Those who spare the rod hate their children" (NRSV). What parent wants to believe he hates his six-year-old daughter? Better use the poor man's weapon against her body.

Proverbs 23:14 says beating one's children saves them from Sheol. The writer did not have in mind the Christian hell. In the Hebrew Bible, Sheol was where everyone ended up after death. Since no one could be saved from it, Proverbs 23:14 employs the word metaphorically for the here-and-now. If children are not beaten with a rod, they will turn out to be lazy, stupid, poor, undisciplined, unteachable, and ungrateful. What parent wants a living hell for a kid?

Proverbs 29:15 is about saving face. Parents do not want to be humiliated when guests come for dinner and their seven-year-old son misbehaves. Avoid being shamed, beat the brat. Better to raise a son full of shame and resentment than for parents to be disgraced. For it has been the universal experience of children that when beaten, they feel degraded, insulted, and rejected. This biblical wisdom can backfire: since children model their parents' behavior, when a child has felt humiliated when spanked, that child may—with growing contempt, resentment, and indifference to physical pain—throw a temper tantrum in front of the guests. Gershen Kaufman says, "Humiliation is a fertile breeding-ground for hatred and for revenge-seeking."

Parental needs are also prioritized over needs of children at Proverbs 29:15. If parents raise foolish children, those children may turn out to be a source of grief and bitterness for them. Parents know what to do so they will not experience these emotions later in life: literally knock some sense into the kid today.

I get the impression Proverbs 23:13 was written for someone who might have objected to beating one's kids. The writer's response, "They will not die" (NRSV). Thrash that four-year-old until she pisses herself. Beat her until she is terrorized and curled up in fetal position. Whip her after you whisper in her ear, "I'm going to beat you to within an inch of your life." But don't worry, you will not beat her to death or hurt her seriously. The Hebrew Bible invested parents with unlimited authority over the bodies of their children. Any sense that it was abuse to beat children until their bodies were broken and bruised did not exist.

Do children benefit from beatings?

In the Book of Proverbs, "they will not die" seems to have been the line parents were not to cross in beating their kids. In *The New Dare to Discipline*, James Dobson feels the line should be drawn elsewhere. For him, it is open season so long as the physical force will "very likely" not cause "permanent damage" or result in a visit to "the emergency room at Children's hospital." It appears damaging a child is acceptable so long as it does not result in permanent physical damage that can be seen.

James Dobson discourages slapping the face, shaking, and yanking the child hard by the arms. And he absolutely forbids doing these actions, including spanking, before a child reaches fifteen to eighteen months of age. He says parents will be "doing it right" by spanking in the "buttocks area." He recommends using a "neutral object" like a "switch or paddle" instead of the hand. His reason: "The hand should be seen as an object of love—to hold, hug, pat and caress." I guess James Dobson supposes five-year-old daughters cannot link the rod to the hand holding it.

James Dobson offers a second reason to dissuade you as a parent from using your hand to spank, and instead, use a switch, paddle, or something like that. He says if you use your hand, your child "can develop a pattern of flinching when you suddenly scratch your head. This is not a problem if you take the time to get a neutral object." For him, flinching is the problem. It is physical damage that can be seen. But what James Dobson fails to observe is that a child flinches because the child has been traumatized. And it does not matter whether the spanking is administered to the body of a child with the rod of the Book of Proverbs, James Dobson's "switch or paddle," or the hand. It traumatizes the child. It is this emotional trauma that finds its voice in bodily flinching. A child usually heals from contusions, lacerations, welts, and bleeding wounds. Emotional trauma leaves permanent scarring.

For James Dobson, there is only one effective way to address a child's "defiant," "stiff-necked," "disrespectful," "unsubmissive," "sassy," "selfish behavior," and "temper tantrums." To obtain an obedient child, the child's behavior has to be met head-on with physical pain. Most everyone concedes that in the short-term a thrashing or spanking works to get compliance to parental authority. Alice Miller says it well in *Breaking Down the Wall of Silence*, "Hammering at this creature as they would a piece of metal, they finally got the obedient robot they wanted." For some parents, a compliant, obedient, and submissive child is precisely what they want, and if they get it, the child turned out fine. A source of enormous pride is the applause parents receive from other parents on how well-behaved their kids are. But how can the unseen fear, degradation, shame, and resentment generated in the heart of a child be beneficial to their character formation?

A father can spank if he wants to be a role model to his four-year-old son, to teach him that, as Beverly Engel says in *Breaking the Cycle of Abuse*, "those more powerful have a right to dominate those who are weaker than themselves." By spanking his son, he communicates that inflicting physical pain is acceptable for managing people and solving problems. His son will reason that if daddy can hit him to curb his naughty behavior, he can imitate daddy when necessary. It is hypocritical to be intolerant of behavior in children that parents tolerate in themselves. Daddy should consider himself rewarded when his son's education kicks in, and he hits a girl as a means to problem solve on the playground. Violence does not result from kids being kids; it is for the most part learned behavior (chapter 13).

His four-year-old son's learning, in fact, goes deeper than mere thinking. To be sure, just as practicing killing trains a soldier to kill, so being hit trains a child to hit. But there is a difference. For soldiers, the conditioning must be repetitive, over and over. But for children, because they so entirely identify with and are attached to their parent, and because it is beyond their comprehension to believe their daddy or mommy is capable of wrong, the conditioning is virtually instantaneous. The education that beating a child communicates needs little repetition to stick.

Does this mean every spanked child turns violent? Of course not. But spankings ignite feelings of degradation, insult, and rejection, emotions that get suppressed in rooms of the child's heart. This buried "humiliated fury" hijacks the impulse to aggression in anger (chapter 10) and triggers anger easier, faster, and more intensely. It is just a matter of where the destructiveness is directed. Some children take the humiliation, shame, and learned violence that comes with the beatings and they turn it inward against themselves. But because this activity is unseen, parents can go on believing their obedient little robot turned out fine. And some children will become emotionally, physically, sexually, and verbally violent to others (chapter 13). All this gets more virulent as the person ages. Emotional resources available to a teen and young adult to keep a lid on suppressed emotions diminish as he or she grows older (chapter 4).

A father says his spankings benefit his seven-year-old son because he does it out of love. It is as though saying it makes it so. But hitting a child with good intentions is no different from hitting a child as a means of meeting the parent's need to feel power over the child. How will his son distinguish a "doing it right" spanking from a vicious spanking that vents pent-up frustration? Both will be pain-filled and result in crying unless the boy is bullied into suppressing his emotions because dad threatens to give him "a little more of whatever caused the original tears." The quoted words belong to James Dobson, who recommends dishing out more physical pain to quench prolonged crying. The little boy learns it is in his best interests to suppress his emotions and live in emotional isolation. You will never see him cry like a little girl. He will grow up with a lot of resentment, sadness, and shame stored inside his body. Out of touch with his own emotions, he will be unable to cultivate deeper, more meaningful relationships with others.

Is the use of a rod loving but a kick abusive? What about a caning stick? Are thirty spankings with the father's bare hand on her bare bottom loving but fifty excessive? For sure, some will object that it is inappropriate for a father to spank his seven-year-old daughter on her bare bottom with his bare hand. For lots of females and males, that "buttocks area" is a place of sexual stimulation. Some fathers will be sexually aroused by spanking their girl's bare bottom and a few children will learn to connect sexual pleasure and pain. But her father might respond to the one who criticizes him, "It's appropriate and loving discipline. It's what seems right to me. Millions of Judeo-Christian fathers have been spanking the bare bottoms of their daughters for centuries. And let me tell you, my bare hand hurts her a whole lot less than a switch or paddle!" James Dobson recognizes parents disagree on this technique stuff and so he encourages parents "to do what seems right to them." He only adds, "It is not a critical issue to me."

Another parent will say, "My kids turned out just fine and I spanked them." Of course, that is true but just so long as "fine" is limited to obedience with no permanent physical damage or trips to the hospital, and leaves unseen and unspoken the degradation, humiliation, and shame.

James Dobson has tremendous faith in the ability of parents to be rational, in control of their emotions and behavior, and spank their kids "according to very carefully thought-out guidelines." But can a father who cannot keep his own temper under control one hundred percent of the time or a mother under a lot of stress hit moderately and reasonably every time? Even if there were such a thing as moderate and reasonable violence against a child's body, physical force escalates instantly when fueled by the parent's anger and suppressed humiliation. When this happens, can the beating result in liver, kidney, or spleen damage?

Parents who believe spanking is acceptable need to feel empathy toward the child—put themselves in the child's place—every second while hitting the child so the beating does not escalate and turn vicious. But each of us knows from personal experience that emotions like anger and frustration effortlessly push empathy aside. As the parent angrily hits the child, the anger feeds off the physical force and the parent feels less and less empathy as the spanking continues. I am curious, have any mothers and fathers who have beaten their kids ever blamed their kids for any unforeseen consequences that result from the spanking turning excessive?

James Dobson sees things differently. He says parental anger will spiral out of control resulting in child abuse when parents do not spank. He says, "There are those in the Western world who will not rest until the government interferes with parent-child relationships with all the force of law." And when governments meddle, he says, "It will be a sad day for families. Child abuse will increase, not decrease, as frustrated parents explode after having no appropriate response to defiant behavior."

James Dobson says that when a father cannot vent his frustration while spanking his four-year-old daughter, his anger will just keep building up inside him. Like a pot boiling over, the father will eventually explode. All manner of abuse will then break loose against the body of the child. For James Dobson, the father's anger and frustration need to find release. For him, it is in the father's best interests to spank his daughter until his emotions are released. He says anger and frustration will not dissipate so long as parents cannot employ the "appropriate response to defiant behavior," namely, hitting the child with a "switch or paddle" in the "buttocks area" or other "constructive, positive forms of physical punishment," whatever "seems right" to the parent.

In *Breaking the Cycle of Abuse*, Beverly Engel uncovers the assumption that leads people like James Dobson to say parents must beat their kids, so their anger and frustration do not build up and explode in abusive behavior against their children. But where James Dobson speaks of anger and frustration, Beverly Engel speaks of anxiety: "Historically, the routine use of children as poison containers to prevent adults from feeling overwhelmed by their anxieties has been universal. Examples from the history of childhood regularly reveal children were expected to absorb the bad feelings of their caregivers."

According to James Dobson, a child must absorb the parent's frustration, anxiety, and anger when spanked so that the parent will not feel overwhelmed and explode. And, given this logic at work in *The New Dare to Discipline*, if the parent cannot release this emotional pressure, it will be a sorry day for the child. But all this puts an exclamation mark on what Paul Ekman says in *Emotions Revealed*: "When violence achieves a useful purpose, few people condemn it."

A parent's emotions, whether anxiety, anger, or frustration, are normal and healthy emotions. Contrary to what James Dobson teaches, parents walking a path of emotional health never need a child's body to manage their own emotions. They take full responsibility for their emotions. They process their emotions and express them in ways that benefit the child's character formation and their relationship with their children.

Soldiers have to dehumanize and depersonalize the enemy so they can kill them. Likewise, parents must erect moral and social distance between themselves and their children to justify inflicting physical pain on their bodies. The Book of Proverbs teaches that children are thick in the head, and their hearts are filled with evil and foolishness. The way to drive that wickedness out of them is to beat it out of them. Based on a lifetime of work with families where child abuse was present, in *Breaking the Cycle of Abuse*, Beverly Engel concluded, "Parents who have a negative perception of their children are far more likely to end up abusing them than parents who have a positive view of their children."

A better way

When I look at the contours of what Jesus taught and how he interacted with children, I see a positive view of children. He felt adults would benefit from emulating children in specific character-building ways (Matthew 18:3–4). Jesus' teaching is at odds with any thinking that sees children as stiff-necked, belligerent, depraved, and in need of a thrashing. There is no hint Jesus felt children were worse sinners than adults. Jesus erased any moral and social distance that existed between adults and children.

Jesus expected people to extend the same value to children they extended to him. Jesus was talking about real children when he said, "Whoever welcomes a child such as this in my name welcomes me" (Matthew 18:5). Jesus was extending rights and respect to children and their bodies. It becomes impossible for me to think Jesus tolerated child abuse in any of its multifarious expressions. Jesus saw how incredibly vulnerable children were. For Jesus, parenting is stewardship, not ownership.

In commenting on Proverbs 13:24, Tremper Longman says, "Parents are motivated to do the *hard work* of correction" (emphasis added). Hard work? Beating one's kids as a means of establishing what James Dobson calls "effective parental authority" is the easy path. It can be unbelievably hard, but thankfully not impossible, to raise children—consistently day in and day out and especially when one does not feel like it—without resorting to spankings and beatings (and yelling and shaming).

If you are a parent or plan to be one, I hope you will weigh seriously the arguments put forward in this chapter. I hope you will rule out the use of physical pain against the body of your child. That means no banging her head against a wall or table, belting, biting, boxing his ear, caning, choking, or hitting. It excludes kicking, pinching, pulling hair, punching, pushing, putting her in a sack and beating the sack, or rapping him on the head. Ruling out physical pain means no shaking, slapping, spanking, throwing her to the ground or across the room, thumping fingers, yanking arms, and anything else I've missed.

If, however, a father says to his daughter, I love you, and then—with free and easy access to her body—spanks her, she might, once she starts dating, tolerate her boyfriend saying the same words and hitting her. The daughter may reason that since this is how her father treated her, her boyfriend can treat her the same way. Her father did not give her the right to say no when she did not want her father to touch her body. She will think she does not have the right to say no when she does not want her boyfriend to touch her. Spanking overrides the child's right to say to another individual, *you have no right to touch my body without my permission*. Should a father and mother treat their daughter's body the way they would want a future boyfriend or husband to treat her body? Should they teach her, by word and example, that her body belongs to her, that she has a right to physical privacy and has the right to say no to unwanted touch?

Raising kids and disciplining them without resorting to physical pain takes truckloads of emotional energy. Thankfully, parents walking a path of emotional health have enough emotional energy, and they can effectively address their child's inappropriate behavior and consistently enforce boundaries.

The goal of parenting is never to break or crush a child's will. When parents release their child to the world as a late teen (even if they stay at home), their young adult children will benefit from a firm will so that they can act on their dreams. But a broken and crushed will can result in a young adult with lots of aspirations and little gritty ambition to realize them.

I can connect the dots between a beating and the coerced obedience that endures for as long as the child fears the parent. I cannot connect the dots between the use of physical force against her body and the nurturing of problem solving skills valuable for decision-making and for managing impulses and emotions as she grows. Parents can model life skills that will serve their children well as adults. Discuss boundaries, own problems together, negotiate, allow your children to assert their ideas, and agree upon effective discipline for when clearly articulated boundaries have been crossed. The more time you spend with your children and know them, the more you will know what effective discipline will look like.

It takes wisdom, sensitivity, patience, reflection, and self-control to figure out what non-violent means are at our disposal and what is uniquely suitable for disciplining our children. And every parent is unique too. Personally, I never used housework as a form of discipline since I did not want Graham to think cleaning his room or picking up his clutter was punishment.

James Dobson rightly says that "many confrontations can be avoided" simply by having more time together with your kids, "having fun together and enjoying mutual laughter and joy." Neglected children act up to get attention. I came away from reading *The New Dare to Discipline* thinking that James Dobson was himself emotionally neglected as a child by his pastor father. This resulted in behavioral problems that lasted until part way through his first year of high school. By his own admission, spankings did not work on him. Only the threat of his mother publicly shaming him worked (chapter 12). How might his childhood years have been different had he had a father who chose to spend time with him, value him, and take a genuine interest in him?

For sure, in a battle of the wills, the parent's will needs to win. But this can happen without the child ever ending up black and blue, or humiliated. Not every disagreement or difference of opinion needs to be interpreted as a challenge to parental authority and become a battleground. Prudent parents pick their battles.

17

Joy

A Satisfyingly Creative Way of Life

WE HAVE COVERED THE practical benefits of managing anger, fear, sadness, and shame for traveling a path of emotional health and self-leadership, foundational for cultivating deeper, more meaningful relationships and friendships with ourselves and others. Just as vital is the nurturing of positive emotions like contentment, fascination, hope, joy, love, thankfulness, and wonder. When we deliberately foster positive emotions, we will have remarkably more success in dealing with negative emotions, and we will—to borrow the title of Martin E. P. Seligman's book—flourish.

Or, if you prefer that murky, overused, generic, and vague word, you will be happy (thanks to Barbara L. Fredrickson's book, *Positivity*, for the adjectives). But consider this. Even though the Greek word for happiness was as common across the ancient Mediterranean as our English word is for us, yet never once does the word occur in the Greek New Testament. It is as though the New Testament writers went out of their way to avoid it. Granted, the word can be absent and the idea present. But still. Maybe that vague word did not take the New Testament writers where they wanted to go, any more than asking—this is my answer to the question I raised in chapter 14—whether Abraham Lincoln was happy takes us anywhere in trying to make sense of the enigma of his life. I am happy to dispense with the word happiness and in its place, offer joy.

How we nurture joy and love—center stage in this and the final chapter—can serve as a template or map for how we promote other positive emotions in our lives, necessary for a life that flourishes.

Joy: an emotional response to favorable circumstances

This is how we typically think of joy. At the emotional high end of the spectrum, joy is an entirely ecstatic and hedonistic emotion. Psalm 126 captures something of this intensely alive, bacchanal emotion. The poet said that when good fortune rained down on them, they rejoiced: "We were like those who dream. Then our mouth was filled with laughter, and our tongue with shouts of joy" (NRSV).

Each of us has experienced this same joy as a satisfyingly pleasant emotional response to favorable circumstances.

The Book of Ezra illustrates how joy as an emotional response to favorable circumstances is delightfully contagious and infectious. The writer says that after the builders finished the foundation of the massive Jerusalem temple, they had a lively celebration. I can imagine their jubilation magnetically attracting a gigantic crowd. Recall Daniel Goleman's "neural wifi" from chapter 2. This rapturous, exhilarating contagion called joy was magnified and intensified when shared (Ezra 3:10–11). Joy is hedonistic but not selfish. When joy explodes in our hearts, we want others in our heart. We spread the feeling. But joy is more than an ecstatic and hedonistic emotional response to favorable circumstances.

The pursuit of the core value of joy

Joy can be sought after. I am not imagining we prime an emotional pump to feel continuously fabulous. Neither do I think we should strive to feel joyful all the time, and when we do not, hit the switch and feel cheery again. Like every other emotion, joy comes and goes. Rather, I am pointing in the direction of nurturing the core value of joy: the firm root of joy that can flourish down below our feelings of joy and all other emotions. This firm root provides nutrients to joy and sadness and makes their friendship deep and comforting.

Consider doing the following six activities for their own sake and to cultivate the core value of joy deep in your heart.

1. Rejoice with those who rejoice

Paul gives his readers practical advice for flourishing: "Rejoice with those who rejoice" (Romans 12:15). Putting this wisdom into practice can be as simple as choosing to celebrate the successes and accomplishments of friends and family, regardless of how we feel.

In the narrative of the Book of Ezra that we looked at above, we saw how people gladly embraced joy. But Ezra says others were milling about who were not so predisposed (Ezra 3:12–13). Ezra says that despite the festival of celebration, this group experienced another emotion, sorrow, and to such a degree they could not contain their anguish. They wept openly and cast a chill over the festivities. Ezra tries to be decent about it. He puts on a happy face and tosses them a bone: they carried on this way because they had seen the former temple of Solomon.

Pretend Ichabod is one of that group. He has a room in his heart filled with joyless pangs of sorrow when he reminisces about Solomon's temple. These aching memories have heartfelt meaning to him. Nothing wrong there. During the many long months of construction on the temple's foundation, Ichabod can choose to respect and take his emotional pain seriously. As he gives himself all the time necessary to process his grief, a deeper joy will quietly slip into that room in his heart and give his sadness lots of hugs. After all, as we saw in chapter 14, joy and sadness play well together. Accompanied now by joy-sadness, Ichabod can choose to rejoice with those who are rejoicing and embrace the celebration.

Back in reality, that is not what happened. They chose to do what Tal Ben-Shahar in *Happier* says is the "one easy step to *un*happiness." They did nothing. They did not answer the door when joy came knocking. They let their gloom and misery run unmanaged during the months of construction and in the end missed out on a fantastic day of joy and celebration. One group was already primed for joy and when there was cause to celebrate, they opened the door and let it in. The other group allowed all their unprocessed emotional clutter to muffle times for gladness. Joy withers in an untended garden. Had Ichabod and the others chosen to rejoice with those who were rejoicing, joy would have become more firmly rooted deep inside them as a core value, which in turn would predispose them to welcome joy in the future.

2. Splash Schadenfreude with acts of joy

We taste this sweet honey when we wish for, stand by and watch, or act to bring about a person's suffering, misfortune, or downfall. "Far sweeter than a stream of flowing honey" is how Homer described this feeling. So universal to human experience is this malicious joy that the German language has a word for it, *Schadenfreude*. English has to make due with quotes. My favorite is attributed to Gore Vidal: "It is not enough that I succeed—others must fail."

Another exception to the rule, *Schadenfreude* is not an emotion that is our friend. We cannot get to a place where we never feel it, but we can manage it. That means no denying, suppressing, or covering it with self-righteousness. As uncomfortable as this can sometimes be, we can take hold of our feelings and thoughts of malicious joy and pause to figure out how intensely we feel *Schadenfreude* and what triggered it. We will probably see clutter inside us that needs attention.

Consider splashing *Schadenfreude* with acts that characterize joy. Send a congratulatory text or card, throw a party, treat your friend or colleague to lunch to celebrate her award or promotion. It is wonderful when our joyful feelings lead our behavior; other times, our behavior has to step up and lead our emotions. Yes, all this sounds rather selfish, even hypocritical: to feel better, act as though you are joyful. Quite the contrary, we act generously because it is not a bad thing to do.

3. Relentlessly communicate thanks

There are times we are so dripping wet with feelings of gratitude that words of thankfulness pour forth spontaneously from our lips. But people who live lives aligned to the core value of thankfulness pour forth words of thanks even when they do not feel particularly thankful. Take every opportunity that comes your way, in fact, be obsessive, to communicate thanks in word and deed without worrying how you feel. These chosen expressions of thankfulness strengthen your core values of thankfulness and joy. And do not be surprised when, in doing these chosen acts of thankfulness, your heart smiles.

4. Work 3:1 into your daily routine

To cultivate the core value of joy, I do what Barbara L. Fredrickson recommends in *Positivity*: for "every heart-wrenching negative emotional experience you endure," aim to experience "at least three heartfelt positive emotional experiences that uplift you." Of course, I do not count to three and you do not need to either. But Barbara Fredrickson is not hunting elephants in Alaska when she says we need multiple positive emotional experiences to counter one negative emotional experience. In chapter 7, I described the enjoyable changes Barbara Fredrickson introduced into her life and the sorts of things she does on a daily basis to lift herself up emotionally. She did not wait for joy to come to her, she went after it. Do the same, and make sure you take one day each week for touching those things that bring you joy (chapter 8).

5. Never, no, never stop being a Tigger

One hot summer afternoon I was out walking at our family cottage. I passed by a farm and saw two horses galloping freely across the field and through the trees. I could think of only one word to describe what the horses were doing, playing. Play had to have been built into their DNA. Can the same be said of humans? Jerry Seinfeld thinks so, at least for some of them, "A lot of people have this little corner of their brain that wants to play all the time."

The Gospel of John tells us that Jesus turned water into a rather impressive vintage wine at a wedding (John 2:1–11). Upon tasting the new wine, the master of ceremonies commented to Jesus that the good booze is normally set out first and only after people have had two-too-many do they bring out the cheap stuff. But Jesus was not anybody, and I guess Jesus knew what lots of people know instinctually, that weddings—at least some of them—need lubrication to be fun.

My point is not to encourage increased alcohol consumption. My point is, Jesus rejected abstinence, austerity, and asceticism. That means, if you strangle fun and pleasure to death in your life, you do not have the wisdom of Jesus on your side. He took pleasure turning water into wine.

John the Baptist traveled the different path. He felt that by living a pleasure-free life of austerity, abstaining from certain foods and drinks, separate from contaminating people like tax-collectors and sinners, he would walk a path of righteousness. Given Jesus' carrying on, it is not at all surprising John the Baptist came to doubt Jesus was "the coming one" (Matthew 11:2–6; Luke 7:33–35).

I asked you back in chapter 7 to answer this question, what might a play ethic look like in your life? I hope some sense of an answer is coming into focus. When all is said and done, you have to decide. Are you on the side of Jesus or John the Baptist? Or to quote Randy Pausch, "You just have to decide whether you are a Tigger or an Eeyore."

6. Act creatively

I knew it would not involve regular trips to the local arts and crafts store; apart from that, I had no idea what I was thinking when I decided six years ago to cultivate creativity as a core value. Later, upon reading Ed Catmull's *Creativity, Inc.*, I saw that what I was after was creating in my life what he calls a "healthy creative environment." For the healthy creative environment that Ed Catmull built at Pixar Animation Studios was an extension of the healthy creative environment of his own life.

For sure, some people come into the world wired to learn one thing faster than other things, whether piano, languages, or mathematics, and some are naturally inclined to one of these domains and not others. But decades of ever-burgeoning research on creativity testifies that the threads that contribute to making a person creative are available to everyone and are entirely inside our control. For most of my life, I had told myself it was a gift and I didn't have it. I misled myself. Now I see there are no restrictions on each of us building into our lives a "healthy creative environment." Because creativity comes to expression in how we communicate, plan, love, problem solve, innovate, evaluate, play, and work together, every one of us can act more creatively. In *Creativity*, Mihaly Csikszentmihalyi says, "It is difficult to imagine a richer life." Creativity performs joyfully. Although this healthy creative environment will look differently for each of us, people who act creatively share six common threads.

The thread of loving it. Just as creativity embodies love and gives expression to our passions, so love puts creativity into motion. Some people discover their passions early on; others take years to clear away the clouds and sort things out. I belong to the second group. And it is not like I arrived at a fixed destination once I sorted things out. I would like to make it very plain, sorting things out has become for me a flowing, changing, lifelong journey.

Creative people act creatively because it is fun, but it sometimes takes proficiency before we have fun. Not for all things in life but for some, the better we get, the more we like it. There are exceptions. I excel at admin but it is as satisfying as plucking ear hairs. Thankfully, enjoyment and competence are linked more often than not.

The thread of mastery. Whether the domain is guitar, leadership, or photography, whether you are tackling a hobby or making a career of it, creativity requires considerable learning of skills and knowledge. Mihaly Csikszentmihalyi says, "A person cannot be creative in a domain to which he or she is not exposed. No matter how enormous mathematical gifts a child may have, he or she will not be able to contribute to mathematics without learning its rules." Learning the rules means obsessive thoroughness: mastering and gaining breadth across a domain, to the limited degree this is manageable. This means being teachable, and the way to be teachable is to learn, keep on learning, never stop learning. The payoff Twyla Tharp says in *The Creative Habit* is, "The more you know, the better you can *imagine*."

Creative breakthroughs almost always result from cross-fertilization and stimulation from another domain. What Francis Crick said for science applies to music, art, and every domain: "Hybrid subjects are often astonishingly fertile, whereas if a scientific discipline remains too pure it wilts."

To use an academic metaphor, pursue a major in one domain and a minor in another. "Creative people," Mihaly Csikszentmihalyi says, "are ever alert to what colleagues across the fence are doing."

The thread of challenge everything. Some people say you can poison your creative abilities by overdosing on mastering the domain. Silliness. You poison your creative abilities by suppressing curiosity, playing it safe, and letting your insecurities win. I load an EA Games disk into the console and a minute later my son and I hear the whisper, "Challenge everything." Strong advice for developing gaming skills and living creatively. But it always comes with a price tag attached. Ed Catmull relates the story how, working as a writer, director, and animator, John Lasseter challenged boundaries at Disney. He pitched a cutting-edge animated film and was immediately fired. His artistic vision was too cutting-edge. John Lasseter went over to Pixar and gave the world *Toy Story*.

To expand understanding and look for better ways forward, to explore new outcomes and navigate around 10,000 obstacles, question, question, question, never stop questioning. To create beautiful melodies, break free from the shelter of playing it safe. Rebel a little, maybe more than a little. Do not let yourself be intimidated by chaos, messiness, and loss of control.

Creative people push back against what Ed Catmull calls the "eternal, impediment to our progress: the human resistance to change." Yes, some change feels like breaking bones, but not all. We can step out of our comfort zones, break the routines of our lives, be flexible, and open ourselves to new paths. The more we do, the more we tap inner resolve and strength we did not know existed. I snatched this idea from Mihaly Csikszentmihalyi, "Keep exploring what it takes to be the opposite of who you are." Spontaneously or premeditated, I try to do things out of character for me. I find myself confronted with a choice and have to decide. It takes courage to go left when I normally go right; but afterward, it felt fun. One qualification: Whatever out of character looks like for you, just be able to tell everyone about it on social media the next day.

The thread of grind. Wolfgang Amadeus Mozart said: "People err who think my art comes easily to me. I assure you, dear friend, nobody has devoted so much time and thought to composition as I." Twyla Tharp described his self-discipline: "Nobody worked harder than Mozart. By the time he was twenty-eight years old, his hands were deformed because of all the hours he had spent practicing, performing, and gripping a quill pen to compose."

Thomas A. Edison said creative work was one percent inspiration. More recently, Austin Madison, an animator at Pixar, upped it to three percent. Ed Catmull found particularly uplifting a letter that Austin

Madison wrote. Whether you are an artist or engineer, may it have a courageous effect on you too:

> To Whom It May Inspire: I, like many of you artists out there, constantly shift between two states. The first (and far more preferable of the two) is white-hot, 'in the zone', seat-of-the-pants, firing on all cylinders creative mode. This is when you lay your pen down and the ideas pour out like wine from a royal chalice! This happens about 3% of the time. The other 97% of the time I am in the frustrated, struggling, office-corner-full-of-crumpled-up-paper mode. The important thing is to slog diligently through this quagmire of discouragement and despair. Put on some audio commentary and listen to the stories of professionals who have been making films for decades going through the same slings and arrows of outrageous production problems. In a word: PERSIST. PERSIST in telling your story. PERSIST on reaching your audience. PERSIST on staying true to your vision.

Whether one or three percent, no matter. At least ninety-seven percent of what creativity requires is persistent tenacity, dogged endurance, and grit. The teenage girl learning the piano disciplines herself, grinds away, sets high expectations for herself, and sits down to practice, no matter her mood. In *Great by Choice*, Jim Collins says, "Without discipline there'd be no chance to do creative work." We consistently grind away, climb over high walls of discouragement, disappointment, and failure, and seek out lots of hugs. And when we reach the point of exhaustion, we rest and recharge, for when exhausted, we do not think or work well.

The thread of failure. You might think I had a few too many dodgeballs to the head in gym class to be discussing failure in a chapter on joy. Bear with me. Ed Catmull tells the story of how Steve Jobs bought Pixar from LucasFilm in 1986 and for a decade poured millions of his own money into Pixar to keep it afloat. This went on until *Toy Story*. Steve Jobs then told Ed Catmull and his team to take the company public so people could buy shares in Pixar. Steve Jobs wanted the movie studio to be on a firm financial footing so that when a movie flopped, the studio could get back on its feet. "The underlying logic of his reasoning shook me," Ed Catmull says. "We were going to screw up, it was inevitable." Steve Jobs taught him that failure is "an inevitable consequence of doing something new." Consider what Ed Catmull learned, "If you aren't experiencing failure, then you are making a far worse mistake: *You are being driven by the desire to avoid it*. And this strategy—trying to avoid failure by outthinking it—dooms you to fail."

A healthy creative environment includes learning to endure failure, repeatedly. And it gets much worse: failure happens when we put everything into it. Failure can be a harrowing nightmare of despair because creativity expresses who we are and what we love. The fear of failure paralyzes and kills creativity like nothing else. It is natural to be terrified of failing, but some people are so afraid of taking risks and failing they never try anything new. I was once like this. Courage and creativity do not melt the fear away. Thomas A. Edison gave himself permission to fail by repackaging how he appraised failure. He said, "I have not failed. I've just found 10,000 ways that won't work." In *Understanding Creativity*, John S. Dacey and Kathleen H. Lennon said, "Creative persons are able to frame their experience in a positive light. All of them face failures in the course of their careers. Each time, they have taken the experience and reframed it in a useful direction. This constructive viewpoint motivates creators to go further because they can build a more successful story for themselves."

We can do the same. We can learn to manage our fears so they do not get in the way of working creatively. It means taking hold of our fears (chapter 4) and listening to what they are trying to tell us (chapter 5). Sometimes, our fears have something valuable to tell us. They can warn us there may be something hazardous or dangerous in front of us. It would be reckless in these situations to close our eyes to fear's cautious wisdom and tell ourselves, "Do not fear." But other times, fear's message can be like the voice of shame. Fear can twist our thinking. It tries to persuade us to do nothing. In times like this, we can be scared to death and saddle up anyway.

Thread of traveling companions. I said the healthy creative environment at Pixar was an extension of Ed Catmull's own life. I was half right. Ed Catmull did not get there by going alone. He collaborated with a team that included, among others, Brad Bird, Pete Doctor, Steve Jobs, John Lasseter, and Andrew Stanton. They loved working together in an environment where job titles and hierarchy were meaningless, and where they had terrific chemistry dreaming, laughing, goofing off, and working hard at what they loved to do. Of course, a lot of solitary work was involved, but they were first and foremost a team. They did not get there by going alone. Pixar Animation Studios was their love story. The romantic myth of the creative genius working entirely alone in complete isolation does not match reality. Build a team, get a mentor, find someone who supports you, loves you, and believes in you. We will not touch our creative potential over the long haul of life on our own. I know I will not.

Joy's desire moves us to silence and awe, thankfulness and generosity. Our joy transforms pain-filled memories and frostbitten feelings. It embraces heartache, kisses a thousand tears, and gives the amethyst sunrise of a mended heart. Joy can't be stilled; it opens our eyes and lifts us to a better place, to create beauty out of darkness and climb mountain peaks and shout, for the whole world to hear, I love you.

18

Love

Where There is No Sacrifice

I'm in-love with you and I love you

MOVIES THE WORLD OVER tell us to let our feelings of being in-love guide us in a romantic relationship and in deciding upon a marriage partner. And it is not just movie scripts. Take Ba Jin's *Family*, a satisfying, semi-autobiographical novel about a family's turbulent life together in the 1920s. We read how young people in Chengdu, China will marry for romantic love, if only they had a say in the matter. If "many waters cannot quench love, neither can floods drown it," then it is no surprise people the world over desire to marry because they feel in-love. These quoted words, taken from that one erotic poem in the Bible, speak un-allegorically of sexual passion, bodily delight, and feelings of being in-love (Song of Solomon 8:7, NRSV).

The rapturous pleasure and sensuous desire, the longing and consuming ecstasy, the obsession and jealousy, the ache, anguish, and possessiveness drives lovers crazy. In-love's magical spell is so intoxicating, it explains why lovers pledge love for always, forever, until we die. And it is why we fail to keep separate *I'm in-love with you* and *I love you*.

When I have walked beside a couple doing pre-engagement or pre-marriage counseling, I begin the first session with two questions. I mentioned the first in chapter 1. Of the fifty to sixty percent of marriages that stay together, how many are satisfying? The second is, how does *I love you* differ from *I'm in-love with you*? The puzzled facial expressions I get tell me most have not thought they are different.

Then I say that most issues that lead to marital breakdown are seen while dating. Love is not blind; couples in-love see each other's faults. But the emotional high of being in-love makes it easy for couples in dysfunctional dating relationships to ignore, postpone, or minimize problems. On the other hand, those intent on building a close friendship—an excellent foundation for lasting marital intimacy—together take responsibility for their problems and work to problem solve. Dating is the time to start these habits, and it signals that each is committed to building a healthy relationship.

The thing is, our feelings of in-love, like all other emotions, have the permanency of a passing breeze. The romantic feelings last a couple days, weeks, months, or years, but they do not last, nor can they. The feelings of in-love are caused by a cocktail of hormones inside our bodies. Eventually our bodies readjust and return to a normal state. Once this happens, those overlooked problems scream for attention: how could I not have seen it before? Well, we did; we just chose to ignore it. And if the *I love you* kind of love does not dwell deeper in the heart, there is little left.

There is nothing wrong with being in-love. But just remember, when our in-love feelings become overwhelming, it gets harder to keep our feet on the ground. We can compromise core values. When this happens, it is hard to think of these feelings of in-love as a friend.

For sure, *I love you* and *I'm in-love with you* overlap. Both can be expansive in generosity. Gifts, dinners, holidays, and finding all the time in the world to be together are a few of the countless ways people express their magnanimous feelings. But if the generosity withers when the feelings of in-love fade, how much *I love you* was there to begin with?

Differences between *I'm in-love with you* and *I love you* become clear when we stop to think about it. The weightiest difference is, *I'm in-love with you* is pure, unmixed emotion, all the way down. Similarly, *I love you* has a robust and vibrant emotional ingredient. But *I love you* is so much more than emotion. As mentioned above, the feelings of being in-love end. Since feelings of in-love are often seen as the reason to date or marry, it is not surprising how many people break off relationships when they no longer feel in-love. Because the feelings of *I'm in-love with you* are just that, feelings, and do not last, being in-love is a bad reason for deciding on a marriage partner.

The emotional ingredient in *I love you* can be intensely joy-filled. As you give each other more access to rooms in each other's hearts and your friendship grows (chapter 1), so also the all-embracing emotional intimacy and feelings of oneness deepen. This is wonderful, but the emotional ingredient depends entirely on other ingredients in *I love you*. To these, we turn shortly.

Nor is it that *I love you* is unselfish and *I'm in-love with you* selfish. Things are never so black-and-white. Take that girl whose boyfriend was a pastor (chapter 9). He hardly saw her because he was "giving it all to God." Was she inappropriately selfish in asking for time together? Or take Diane (chapter 10). She labored for years to get her husband's attention so they could address problems in their marriage. Was she inappropriately selfish?

To be sure, the *I'm in-love with you* kind of love can be incredibly selfish and narcissistic in ways the *I love you* kind of love can never be. When gifts come, they can come with hooks attached; something is expected in return. A young woman told me how she and her boyfriend became lovers. I knew the inner workings of their relationship and instantly thought that what she meant was, they became users. He used her body for his gratification and she used his for hers, and she called it love.

Let me highlight one more difference. *I love you* can be a core value (chapter 5), whereas *I'm in love with you* can never be. As a core value, love is strengthened in the same way we nurture other core values, by doing acts of love regardless of how we feel. When we have love as a core value, our behavior and emotions will align with it. And the core value of love powerfully shapes how we experience all other emotions.

Love loves the light

When we have truth as a core value, truth can keep love in the light. For in the light is where love flourishes and never fails. Truth protects and preserves the life of a relationship and the life of the relationship is love. When love stumbles or slides toward shadows—for there is no such thing as perfect love or perfect people this side of the moon—truth can lead love back to the light. When truth is a core value, we can come to a place where it is impossible to lie to the person we love, so deep is our love for that one person.

Jesus spent his time with the wrong people—tax collectors and sinners, the dispossessed, oppressed, and marginalized, those without money, status, and power, the invisible in the eyes of the influential and strong—loving, touching, and welcoming their touch and love. They were attracted to Jesus because in the light of his presence they were safe, accepted, and valued, each a mark of *I love you*. The religious leaders set themselves on exterminating Jesus because they took offense at how he loved.

Killing, violence, savagery, inquisitions, censorship, shaming, shunning, character-assassination, excommunication, viciousness, and pious cruelty have always been part of every religious doctrine, political ideology, and social-justice cause that ranks truth and dogma higher than love. Jesus was put to death by people who thought there was something more important than love.

Love that is relentless and vulnerable

So Jesus told them three stories to help them understand what *I love you* is about. These stories are known to us as the Parables of Lost Sheep, Lost Coin, and Lost Son (Luke 15).

Jesus asked, "What person among you who has a hundred sheep and loses one of them, will not leave behind the ninety-nine in the wilderness and go after the one that was lost, taking all the time necessary until it is found?" The answer inside the Parable of the Lost Sheep can only be, "Of course, everyone will leave the ninety-nine sheep in the wilderness and go after the one lost sheep, and that person will not come back until it has been found."

But unless we read into the story details not there, it would be irresponsible, reckless, and careless in a world where every move is calculated and every person judged to abandon the ninety-nine and go after the one lost. We cut our losses and move on. But this parable is about what *I love you* means. It is the kind of love that values one person to such an extent that love would abandon everything to run, pursue, and track down, one person. So relentlessly does *I love you* love just one person.

We see this same love in the Parable of the Lost Son. Some man, Jesus said, had two sons and the younger demanded his father give him the share of the family wealth that fell to him. The father distributed to both sons what each was entitled to. A few days later the younger son took his share and traveled to a land far away. There he wasted the family wealth living in selfishness and debauchery. Immediately upon squandering everything, a severe famine broke out and he began to starve to death. He attached himself to a resident of that land and ended up tending swine (he is Jewish). He hungered to eat what the pigs were eating, but no one gave him anything. He then remembered. All his father's hired men had an overabundance of food. So he made a plan to return to his father and confess how he sinned against heaven and in the eyes of his father. He would say he was no longer worthy to be called his father's son. He would ask to be treated like one of his father's hired men.

Although absent from the story, I effortlessly imagine the father, day in, day out, year in, year out, looking to the distant horizon for his son's return. The father, powerless and exposed, never surrenders. Every day it rains yet he whispers *I love you*. Every moment he waits in hope against hope, with an aching heart, that love will draw him home. *I love you* flows from the unending tears of broken-heartedness. The father's body never readjusts or returns to a normal state. Not in this place. To quote Henri J. M. Nouwen in *The Return of the Prodigal Son*, the father had "to surrender one more time to a love that knows no limits." One more time turned out to be every day.

I asked my best friend once, "Do you believe you could love one person forever? Not the *I'm in-love* kind that withers. Rather, the *I love you* love." I have thought long about this question and for me the answer is yes, and forever is a long time.

Love endures. But does it wobble, shake, totter, and waver? Was there a day when the father was overthrown by his ever-present ache and anguish, by the despair and dark grey, by the uncertainty of crippling doubt? Was there a day when waiting proved too much? Did his longing and consuming desire for the one he loved sometimes make him feel adrift without direction or mooring? Were there moments he lay prostrate on the ground because the seismic shaking of his love made it just too hard to stand? I wonder, was he tempted to take control, become thick-skinned (chapter 7), put something above love, and kill his pain-filled feelings of hope?

In this story, the father's love has a happily-ever-after ending. But as he looked to that distant horizon and waited, day in and day out, there were no guarantees, no inevitabilities. There was nothing except the enduring, unending, unfailing, and unstoppable certainty of his love for the one he loved, even when—in terrifying moments—he felt only barrenness and emptiness. His son was free and not on a leash. The son was not some marionette puppet with Fate, Destiny, Karma, or God sovereignly manipulating the strings off-stage. *I love you* embraces uncertainty, gentleness, and the truth that love freely lets the other go, sometimes every day, and on occasion forever.

The father opened his heart wide and gave his heart to his son without restraint or holding anything back. He showed his younger son where the son could stick the knife to inflict everlasting bleeding and anguish. Unprotected and defenseless, *I love you* involves suffering, always. Sometimes, *I love you* feels like the tears will never end. You wonder how much the human heart can endure. The son could have stayed away. The son could have spat on the father's love, stepped on it, stuffed it back down his throat, or simply just ignored it. His father's love had set him free. Love cannot be a bully or bulldozer.

Looking to the distant horizon, the father caught sight of his younger son while his son was still far away. The father did not worry about what others would think. He ran and threw himself upon his son's neck and kissed him. This is where his extravagant, reckless, relentless *I love you* took him. Loving his younger son was who he was.

And the son's self-assessment of how he was undeserving and unworthy fell on deaf ears; it was an evaluation the father did not share.

The father told his men to go quickly and fetch the long, flowing robe, the best one, and put it on his son. He ordered a ring be placed on his son's hand and sandals for his presumably bare feet. The father then instructed them to kill the fattened calf. They were going to celebrate. *I love you* rejoices extravagantly.

This son whom he loved was dead and now alive, lost and now returned. I wonder, could the same be said of the father? I think so.

The father could have robed himself in a venerable and inviolable reputation or barricaded himself behind dignity, honor, and respect. He could have handed down to his son "for what a person sows, this also he will reap." His religion would have called him a righteous man. But the father was a misfit; he gave himself away without restriction. He chose open wounds. Of this love, C. S. Lewis says in *The Four Loves*:

> There is no safe investment. To love at all is to be vulnerable. Love anything and your heart will be wrung and possibly broken. If you want to make sure of keeping it intact you must give it to no one, not even an animal. Wrap it carefully round with hobbies and little luxuries; avoid all entanglements. Lock it up safe in the casket or coffin of your selfishness. But in that casket, safe, dark, motionless, airless, it will change. It will not be broken; it will become unbreakable, impenetrable, irredeemable. To love is to be vulnerable.

In chapter 12, I said we can shed light on areas of insecurity and vulnerability in our lives, push through some of our insecurities and vulnerabilities, and build character. But *I love you* takes us to a place where we let vulnerability devour us. There we let go of security and control, and we dare to courageously embrace a vulnerability that unhinges us from holding it all together and being self-contained. C. S. Lewis was right, "To love at all is to be vulnerable."

Welcoming love

Call it paradox, antinomy, mystery, call it what you will. But to give your heart away in love, vulnerability, and without restraint to another person, to say *I love you*, is to open your heart to hungering for and needing that other person's love. We love, not from up on a platform or pedestal, but eye-to-eye, hand holding hand, heart pouring itself into another's heart and hands. Love gives generously and, at one and the same time, needs and aches for the other's generosity of love. Each of us has a need deep inside us to love and be loved by another human being. This is the portion of people who feel dirt between their toes, dirt seen here as an incredibly beautiful thing. This is the portion of that father overthrown by love, who, day in, day out, year in, year out, looked to the distant horizon for the return of his younger son.

In that place of vulnerability and suffering, he loved, and he needed to be loved in the physical embrace of his son. I could never have written these words a few years ago.

In his *On Writing: A Memoir of the Craft*, Stephen King tells how he was driving and his wife Tabitha was in the passenger seat reading a draft of his writing that he thought funny. He kept peeking over to see if Tabitha was smiling or giggling. He says, "On my eighth or ninth peak (I guess it *could* have been my fifteenth), she looked up and snapped: 'Pay attention to your driving before you crack us up, will you? Stop being so goddam *needy!*'" Five minutes later Tabitha was laughing and that was all Stephen King needed. He added, "The truth is that most writers *are* needy."

The truth is all humans are needy. As I mentioned in chapter 7, there is nothing wrong with this. But all my life I was brainwashed into thinking that needing the love of another human was a weakness. I was programmed to be independent of love from another person. I felt ashamed of my need to be loved and my longing to be hugged by one other person. I felt it was a sin to want, need, and long for the love of another person. It is a lifelong journey, but I am learning there is nothing wrong with needing and wanting love from another human whom I love to fill every room in my heart. I am learning this truth, loving you is who I am and being loved by you is who I am.

Needing to be loved and being human (chapter 3) are not a prison from which I want to escape anymore. As much as I still want to deny it, I now see that suppressing my normal, healthy human need to be loved actually dams up the flow of my love for the other. So please, no more "God is my sole sufficiency and God is all I need." I am tired of hearing it is selfish and weak to need to be loved by another human. Giving and receiving love, relentlessly with a generous heart and without constriction, is where this book on emotional health leads. That means vulnerability. I love you and want, even need, to be loved.

No love greater than this

To see just how much Abraham was willing to sacrifice for God, God decided to test him (Genesis 22). Would Abraham sacrifice his own son to prove he was terrified of God? Walking to the mountain of filicide, Isaac asked his father where the sacrificial lamb was. The unspoken, truthful answer was, "Isaac, I will slaughter and sacrifice you." While every word that Abraham actually said was true, he misrepresented the truth to his son. Why did he lie? Was he ashamed because he could not put the life of his son ahead of his own?

The logic of fear in this story is straightforward: Abraham, kill your son and sacrifice him to show me you are afraid of what I will do if you do not obey me. Noncompliance carried terrifying consequences. From the story of the sacrifice of Isaac, I can learn something about how sacrificing and fear shape relationships; I learn nothing of love.

For love cannot say, "If you don't love me, I'll make you suffer." Love cannot say, "If you love me, you will sacrifice for me." Neither is love capable of saying, "Look how much I sacrificed for you." Love from one person's heart to the other's heart can generate love, joy, generosity, and thankfulness. Please hear me, love cannot produce fear, debt, obligation, or sacrifice.

There is no sacrifice in love.

Mind you, it is common to use the language of sacrifice in the context of love. Louis Armstrong said, "I was determined to play my horn against all odds, and I had to sacrifice a whole lot of pleasure to do so." And Nelson Mandela said, "Only through hardship, sacrifice and militant action can freedom be won. The struggle is my life. I will continue fighting for freedom until the end of my days." Both gave up much. But how could Louis Armstrong's giving up lesser pleasures be a sacrifice when compared to pursuing the great pleasure and love of playing the trumpet? A similar question can be asked for Nelson Mandela. I do not think the language of sacrifice fits the language of love.

Where there is sacrifice, there is boasting, competition, resentment, duty to pay back, and lots of room for extortion. Jesus did not go there. Jesus did not say, "Look how much I sacrificed for you. Can you now sacrifice for me?" The writer of 1 John did not say, "We sacrifice because Jesus first sacrificed." The writer said, "We love because he first loved us" (1 John 4:19). It was no sacrifice for Jesus to love.

Jesus said, "No one has love greater than this, to lay down one's life for one's friends" (John 15:13). This is what I mean when I say *I love you*. I will lay down my life for you without a moment's hesitation. And there is no sacrifice in this, my love for you. There just isn't.

Parts of the New Testament interpret Jesus' death as a human sacrifice to deal with sin, but it was no sacrifice for Jesus to love. This distinction is so fundamental, so open to confusion with respect to how I understand *I love you*, that I want to repeat it. Jesus' death was presented as a sacrifice for sin. But it was no sacrifice for Jesus to lay down his life in love for those he loved.

I love you neither requires nor needs sacrifice. Loss of sleep, yes, but no sacrifice. Marlene Dietrich said, "It's the friends you can call up at 4 a.m. that matter." If I am your 4 a.m. friend and you reach out to me in the middle of the night, I might involuntarily grumble for a nanosecond (one billionth of a second), but it will not last more than a millisecond. To be at your side in the middle of the night is the place of joy for me. As your 4 a.m. friend, my love for you is unable to interpret getting out of bed and coming to your side as a sacrifice. The brightness you will see in my eyes at 4 a.m. is love alone (to borrow a couple words from Toni Morrison's *Beloved*). Same goes if I fly halfway around the world to be by your side or take a bullet for you.

In fact, as your 4 a.m. friend, I will be filled with sadness if you do not call me, and for one simple reason: I love you, I find joy in loving you, and there is no sacrifice inside this love in my heart for you. Seven billion voices will tell you I'm wrong, but there is no sacrifice in love. To repeat, there just isn't. Brokenness, vulnerability, loss of sleep, and many tears, yes. For suffering is woven deep into the fabric of love, but love does not look upon tears as a sacrifice.

This is what I mean when I say *I love you*. And love is where it all leads.

500 Words for Emotions

Affection

Accepted, adored, cherished, compassionate, concern, craving, desire, empathy, fondness, inflamed with passion, in-love, lovable, love, love-sick, merciful, neediness for affection, passionate, sympathetic, tenderness, treasured.

Agitation

Agony, anxious, apprehensive, bothered, concerned, confused, desperate, devastated, discontented, distraught, distressed, disturbed, edgy, fidgety, flustered, fretful, frantic, frazzled, frenzied, frustrated, harassed, hesitant, horrible, impatient, indecisive, irritated, jumbled, on edge, overwhelmed, perplexed, provoked, rattled, restless, ruffled, shocked, stressed, suffocated, surprise, tense, tormented, trapped, troubled, uncertain, uncomfortable, uneasy, uptight, unnerved, vexed, weighed down, worried, yucky.

Anger

Aggravated, argumentative, belligerent, bitchy, combative, contentious, cross, enraged, exasperated, fed up, furious, hostile, hot-tempered, in a huff, in a rage, incensed, indignant, infuriated, irate, irked, livid, mad, miffed, outraged, peeved, pissed, provoked, seething, testy, ticked off, volatile, worked up.

Arrogance

Boastful, conceited, judgmental, haughty, proud, superior.

Awe

Admiration, amazed, astonished, honored, proud, reverence, veneration, wonder.

Boredom

Ambivalent, apathetic, blasé, drained, exhausted, indifferent, in the doldrums, lazy, listless, mopey, numb, sluggish, uninterested, unmotivated, weary, wiped-out, worn-out.

Confidence

Adventurous, airy, amazing, anticipation, assertive, awesome, bold, bouncy, buoyant, composed, courageous, daring, determined, effervescent, encouraged, energetic, fantastic, full of life, hopeful, inspired, intensely alive, invincible, magnificent, motivated, optimistic, refreshed, revived, secure, self-assured, significant, sparkling, sure, tenacious, terrific, upbeat, valued, vigorous, vivacious, zealous.

Covetousness

Envy, greedy, jealous, selfish.

Disgust

Affronted, appalled, foul, ghastly, horrified, insulted, nauseous, offended, revolting, revulsion, vile.

Excitement

Amused, ardently absorbed, beside myself, curious, eager, enthusiastic, exuberant, fascinated, interested, inquisitive, intrigued, passionate, rapt, thrilled.

Fear

Afraid, alarmed, apprehension, cautious, chicken, cowardly, dread, faint-hearted, fright, guarded, horror, intimidated, nervous, panic, paralyzed, scared, startled, shy, terrorized, threatened, timid, trepidation, wary.

Grumpiness

Annoyed, cantankerous, crabby, cranky, disagreeable, grouchy, irritable, out-of-sorts, prickly, whiny.

Guilt

Bad, contrite, convicted, deplorable, regret, remorse, reprehensible, sheepish, sinful, sorry.

Hatred

Abhorrence, animosity, antagonism, aversion, bitterness, contempt, cruel, destructive, disdain, distaste, enmity, hostility, ill will, loathing, malevolence, malice, mean, mean-spirited, miserly, misogynous, nasty, rancor, repugnance, resentment, revulsion, sarcasm, scorn, spite, stingy, vengeful, venomous, viciousness, vindictive.

Joy

Bliss, cheerful, delight, dreamy, ecstatic, elated, enraptured, euphoria, exhilarated, fabulous, festive, fortunate, full of fun, giddy, glad, gleeful, glowing, happy, jolly, jovial, jubilant, lighthearted, lucky, marvellous, merry, on cloud nine, overjoyed, playful, pleasant, pleased, radiant, rapturous, saucy, sunny, wonderful.

Sadness

Abandoned, aching with sadness, anguish, bereaved, bereft, bleak, blue, broken, broken-hearted, cast off, cheerless, cloudy, crushed, deflated, dejected, depressed, desolate, despair, desperate, despondent, destitute, disappointed, discouraged, disillusioned, dismal, dismayed, dissatisfied, down, downcast, downhearted, dull, empty, forsaken, gloomy, grief, grim, glum, heartbroken, heavy-hearted, homesick, hopeless, hurt, lonely, lost, lousy, melancholy, miserable, moody, morose, mournful, pessimistic, rejected, shattered, somber, sorrow, sullen, torn apart, unfulfilled, unhappy, upset, wretched.

Shame

Ashamed, cheapened, defective, defiled, degraded, demeaned, despicable, diminished, dirty, discarded, disgraced, disparaged, dishonored, disposable, embarrassed, flawed, foolish, humiliated, inferior, insignificant, ludicrous, mortified, painfully self-consciousness, pathetic, put down, ridiculed, ridiculous, rotten, self-disgust, shabby, stupid, unlovable, used, worthless.

Thankfulness

Appreciative, bighearted, generous, grateful, gratitude, magnanimous.

Tranquility

At ease, calm, comfortable, comforted, contentment, mellow, peaceful, relaxed, relief, safe, satisfied, serene.

Vindication

Absolved, avenged, blameless, guiltless, liberated, justified, relieved.

Violation

Abused, betrayed, cheated, defrauded, judged, oppressed, tricked.

Vulnerability

Awkward, helpless, inadequate, inept, insecure, useless.

Individual or Group Study Guide

1

Introduction

Walking a Path of Emotional Health

1. Family, friends, school, colleagues, religion, books, music, television, and movies taught you about emotions growing up. What did you learn?

2. Growing up, were boys and men expected to express emotions differently than girls and women? If so, how?

3. How would you describe your attitude to your emotions?

4. What results from living emotionally unhealthy lives?

5. If you have a relationship where you feel you must wear a mask and not be yourself, why do you think that is?

6. What does it mean to walk a path of emotional health?

7. How might the discussion of Jesus' emotions have relevance to how you think of emotions?

8. Describe the metaphors of rooms in the heart and our lives as a tapestry. How do these metaphors connect to becoming your own best friend?

2

How Emotions Work

1. Why do you think the traditional view of emotions has been so popular throughout human history and in religion and philosophy?

2. If "our emotions, an activity of the brain, are as much a language of communication as our thinking," can you think of times your emotions tried to communicate with you and help you make sense of things?

3. Agree, disagree, why: "lack of emotion, rather than making us smarter, makes us more irrational and can put our lives at risk."

4. What do you think of the idea that emotions enable moral behavior?

5. Discuss: "The longer I walk a path of emotional health, the more I rely on what my emotions are telling me. In fact, I trust my emotions, and when my emotions disturb me, there is often good reason."

6. What is an emotional predisposition? How do we get them? Do you think you might have a disposition toward an emotion? Do you think a person can have an emotional predisposition to joy?

7. Describe the "essential distinction" between the internal emotion, its external expression, and the time-gap in between. What do you think?

8. Discuss: "How we outwardly express our emotions — with rare exceptions — is learned behavior. Because it is learned behavior, every one of us can act responsibly and relearn how to manage and express our emotions."

3

Welcome Back to the Human Race

1. Discuss: "we come to accept ourselves, even like ourselves, as frail, likable, normal, flawed, far-less-than-perfect human beings, profoundly deserving of love and capable of giving love"?

2. Agree, disagree, why: "it was in her place, precisely as the woman caught in adultery, that Jesus opened for her a path for change and growth."

3. How is it that individuals like the sinful woman of Luke 7 can show great love?

4. Why do you think people strive to be perfect? What is wrong with perfectionism?

5. How does the view of integrity put forward in this chapter differ from one that says integrity is striving to live a flawless, blameless, and unblemished life?

6. Discuss: "The curious paradox is that when I accept myself just as I am, then I can change" (Carl R. Rogers).

7. Growing old well is one advantage of walking a path of emotional health. I say, "I believe that in five years, each of us can be noticeably more truthful, joy-filled, creative, generous, and thankful." What do you think?

8. Some religions teach that through faith and prayer, a person can be healed entirely from their traumatic past (as though the trauma never happened). I suggest something more modest, that "we can mend to varying degrees." What do you think?

4

TLC

Take Hold of Your Emotions

1. In what ways do we suppress or bury our emotions? Can you give examples from your life?

2. What are consequences that come from suppressing or burying our emotions?

3. Suppressing our emotions is not effective but even less so as we get older. Why?

4. Discuss: "Why bother laboring at self-leadership and walking a lifelong path of emotional health when you can pop a pill?"

5. What am I getting at when I say we all need some "emotional cocaine"? What is your emotional cocaine?

6. What are the problems with addiction as a way to manage our emotions?

7. Is venting okay?

8. What does it mean to take hold of your emotions?

5

TLC

Listen to Your Emotions

1. Describe a recent emotional experience (Take hold of your emotions). Then ask why you felt the way you did. Or, what were your emotions trying to communicate to you?

2. How are our emotions a "love language" (Gary Chapman's phrase)?

3. What are core values? Why are they important? How do they relate to our emotions and behavior? How do we strengthen and weaken our core values?

4. Can you identify three core values you have? Explain why you selected them? Can you name one core value you want to nurture in your life?

5. Explain: "Our emotions align with these dark core values and, consequently, stop acting as a friend."

6. Agree, disagree, why: "The reality is, we have tremendous capacity for self-deception."

7. How can the emotion of guilt be good for us? When can guilt be toxic?

8. Discuss: "But emotions are slow to learn, and that is why we need to be patient with them as they readjust to our new reality."

6

TLC

Courage to Change

1. Discuss: "Do not underestimate the benefits that come from embracing common daily fears."

2. Agree, disagree, why: "Knowing what needs to be changed and then not doing it restricts our capacity to change in the future."

3. Is God a matchmaker? Explain your answer.

4. What are the problems with "I feel God is" talk?

5. Just how much should we rely on the feeling of peace in decision-making?

6. What do you think of what Sigmund Freud said, "Most people do not really want freedom, because freedom involves responsibility, and most people are frightened of responsibility?"

7. How much can we change? Please feel free to bring in the discussion from chapter 3.

8. Discuss: "Each of us can walk a path to a place where we are free to be fully self-responsible for everything in our lives, including our decision-making and how we express our emotions."

7

Keep Your Heart with All Vigilance

1. I suggest that for a time Paul did not practice what he would later tell leaders, "Give earnest attention to yourselves and all the flock" (Acts 20:28). What were the consequences for him of not practicing healthy self-care?

2. Discuss: "Self-care is never a selfish act – it is simply good stewardship of the only gift I have, the gift I was put on earth to offer others. Anytime we can listen to true self and give it the care it requires, we do it not only for ourselves, but for the many others whose lives we touch" (Parker Palmer).

3. Darwin Smith said, "I never stopped trying to become qualified for the job." What was behind this?

4. "From walking a path of emotional health, I have learned to stop denying I deeply need to receive love, and there is nothing wrong about this." What do you think?

5. When do you think a healthy sense of neediness crosses the line and becomes inappropriate or excessive?

6. What does it mean to narcissistic? Do you know a narcissistic person?

7. Answer the seven questions in the bullets in "Top up your emotional gas tank." Also, describe how you feel and act when your emotional gas tank is topped up and when it is drained.

8. What do you think of the discussion on being thin-skinned?

8

Jesus' Sabbath

Touching Those Things That Bring You Joy

1. This chapter can be for everyone, even though parts of it address Christian concerns. What is Sabbath rooted in Jesus?

2. Discuss: "My favorite way to think of Sabbath is to imagine having one full day every week where you are free to touch those things that bring you joy."

3. Agree, disagree, why: "Sabbath tied to Jesus was not about substituting one kind of work for another. It was not about exchanging secular work for the Lord's work. Jesus never expected Christians would drive themselves to exhaustion by volunteer labor in church work on Sundays."

4. How can you benefit from "having one full day every week where you are free to touch those things that bring you joy"?

5. Discuss: "How might Sabbath look in your life? What obstacles are presently in your life that might get in the way of living this Sabbath?"

6. What do you think of the idea that sometimes we need to take a break from trying to better or improve ourselves?

7. Discuss: "Walking a path of emotional health is not only about managing emotions like anger, fear, sadness, and shame (chapters 10–14). It

is also about encouraging positive emotions like empathy, gratitude, joy, and serenity in our life (chapters 17–18)."

8. Agree, disagree, why: "To be fully present we need to be fully absent."

9

Living inside Boundaries

1. "This 'just can't ever let it go' pattern of overwork, workaholism, and long hours is widespread and esteemed across the globe. It has always been respected in church cultures." Why do you think this is so?

2. In chapter 7, I said, "We carve out time from our full and active lives for the people we love, always." What are the implications of this?

3. How can body weight, eating habits, physical fitness, and sleep patterns adversely impact us emotionally?

4. Discuss: "Some people take their emotional energy and spread it over a normal work week. They work at peak levels of excellence, productivity, and performance. Fanatically driven, they are fully engaged emotionally." Others "are physically at work all the time but only give it seventy-five percent."

5. How is workaholism an addiction? Look back to "Feel better, pop a pill" in chapter 4.

6. How does "giving it all to God" dishonor God?

7. What was the clutter in Moses' life that needed his attention, and how did Jethro help Moses?

8. Imagine what your life would be like in the coming year if you lived within healthy boundaries and limits.

10

The Experience of Anger

1. Some people are energized by getting angry. They feel alive and in control. Others hate the feeling of anger. Where do you place yourself?

2. Is the emotion of anger sin?

3. As a goal for emotional health, should we strive to be anger-free?

4. The story about Diane and her marriage has something to teach us about anger. What is it?

5. Agree, disagree, why: "We get angry about things we hold close to our heart. We get angry because our anger is soaked with core values about what is dear to us."

6. "But way too often, we do not want to hear the message our anger is trying to deliver to us." Why?

7. How prone are you to passive-aggressive behavior?

8. Is yelling acceptable in day-to-day relationships?

11

The Positive Management of Anger

1. Taking full responsibility for our anger is an important first step in putting together a personally tailored, practical strategy for managing anger. What can this look like for you?

2. A proven strategy for managing anger is "take a time-out and regroup." However, once our anger settles down, we can ignore the issue that ignited the anger. How might you address this problem?

3. "We need one or two principles, already programmed into our brains, that will automatically push into our awareness when we get angry." What do I mean? Why is this important? How do we program principles into our brains?

4. Discuss: "For where there are chronically angry people, there you will find toxically competitive cultures, at home, school, and work."

5. Many say anger and love are incompatible. For sure, this applies to suppressed anger and inappropriate expressions of anger. But I suggest anger and love work well together. Who is right and why?

6. "When we get angry, our anger looks for words to match how we feel." And then I say, "Sometimes our anger gets the words right. Other times our anger does not." How so?

7. Discuss: "Anger can create powerful changes in the world. It can be a catalyst for bringing atrocities to light, stamping out injustices, and create new structures and systems to replace those that are corrupt and inadequate. Anger can empower those who have been tyrannized

or victimized, imbuing them to stand up to their oppressors" (Beverly Engel).

8. Agree, disagree, why: "Suppose you have an ongoing, unresolved disagreement with your spouse. Any anger connected to that unresolved disagreement does not go away. It takes up residence in rooms in your heart and festers away as resentment. The passing of time does not diminish it."

12

Shame and the Disintegration of the Self

1. In what ways does shame manifest itself?

2. John Bradshaw says, "One of the devastating aspects of toxic shame is that it is multigenerational." How so?

3. Shame and humiliation are used in parenting the world over. It is an easy way to parent and takes no skill or learning. Does the fact that it works to break a child's will and force compliance to parental expectations justify using it?

4. James Dobson offers his mother's terror tactics as "a better idea" worth emulating. What do you think?

5. How does parental shaming and humiliation affect children and teens?

6. How does comparison work as a weapon of shaming?

7. Some shame researchers think all shame is bad. Others think it has a limited positive role. The story of Tamar illustrates the positive role. Tamar feels shame that anticipates future shame, and it motivates her to act to prevent the rape. How do you come down on this controversial issue?

8. What is the difference between guilt and shame? How does shame hijack guilt?

13

The Humiliated Fury of Buried Shame

1. How might buried shame and addiction be inseparable?

2. What are some ways people deal with their buried shame? Which strategies can you relate to?

3. Where would you draw the line between acceptable and inappropriate people-pleasing?

4. Agree, disagree, why: "Anger and rage can insulate a person, including children, against the painful, destabilizing feelings of shame," and "Underneath much violent behavior in children and youth is buried shame."

5. How can buried shame get in the way of love?

6. How are buried shame and addiction to power linked?

7. Bring together the comments on perfectionism in the section "Integrity" in chapter 3 with the comments on perfectionism in this chapter. What is the problem with perfectionism? How does buried shame drive perfectionism?

8. Discuss: "In excavating and exposing our buried shame and all the painful memories down there in rooms in our heart, we learn to tell our own story. Somewhere along the way we come to see and accept that we are enough."

14

Sadness

Music for Those Who Listen

1. Take a moment to reread the story of Marie, a dear friend of mine from years ago, in the section "There's no problem so big that I can't run from it" in chapter 4. Why do you think we do not give ourselves and others permission to allow the tears to fall?

2. Agree, disagree, why: A lot of martyrdoms are suicides in disguise.

3. An idea that connects chapters 14 and 17 is how sadness and joy can be friends and work well together. What do you think?

4. In what ways did Nehemiah and Geri Scazzero need and benefit from sadness?

5. How do you respond to the portrait of Job's depression and despair?

6. In chapter 13, I said, "Self-slaughter is where buried shame, from the trauma of abuse and hopelessness of despair, takes many thousands of girls and women in China every week who kill themselves." Given that many girls and women in China (and around the world) "are treated as inferior, subordinate, subservient, less significant, less valued, and less than equal to males," the resulting resentment, despair, and depression can be contributing factors to self-violence. What do you think?

7. "Abraham Lincoln ransomed his depression and it gave him clarity, discipline, and hope. He integrated his depression into his life and it

fueled his mission as a leader. But Abraham Lincoln never got better." How might integrating sadness across the tapestry of our lives sometimes be more necessary or valuable than getting over it?

8. The metaphor of holding on to a baseball can be applied to every emotion. What is the point of the metaphor in relation to sadness?

15

The Hideous Chamber of Horrors Called Abuse

1. Discuss: "In every culture for all recorded history, the extent of abuse has been so astronomical, so pervasive, so pandemic, of such magnitude. Statistics underestimate how widespread abuse is."

2. Why do many people underestimate the effects of the abuse?

3. Reread the narratives of Alice Miller (chapter 4), Selena (chapter 5), and Beverly Engel (this chapter) on the abuse they suffered. What lessons can we learn?

4. Discuss: "Parents inflict most child abuse. Many parents do not think their behavior is abuse. And sadly, many cultures encourage children, teens, and adults to keep a lid on the painful emotions and memories of the abuse they suffered as children."

5. What do I mean when I talk about assigning appropriate blame? How does assigning appropriate blame connect to taking responsibility?

6. I argue that honoring one's parents does not shield parents from appropriate blame if they have abused their children. What do you think?

7. What is spiritual abuse?

8. What is defensive hope? What is the problem with it? Do you think there should be limits to hope?

16

On the Spanking and Beating of Children

1. To what extent are you persuaded by this chapter's arguments that beating the bodies of children does not benefit their character formation?

2. The Book of Proverbs seems to say "they will not die" is the line not to cross when beating children. James Dobson says the line is no "permanent damage" or visits to "the emergency room at the Children's Hospital." Tremper Longman puts it at "hurt seriously." If you think spanking and hitting children is appropriate, where do you draw the line?

3. Agree, disagree, why: "Violence does not result from kids being kids; it is for the most part learned behavior."

4. James Dobson tells parents to dish out "more physical pain to quench prolonged crying." I respond, "The little boy learns it is in his best interests to suppress his emotions and live in emotional isolation. You will never see him cry like a little girl. He will grow up with a lot of resentment, sadness, and shame stored inside his body. Out of touch with his own emotions, he will be unable to cultivate deeper, more meaningful relationships with others." What do you think?

5. James Dobson says child abuse will increase if parents are not permitted to vent their frustration while spanking their children. I argue, "No parent walking a path of emotional health ever needs a child's body to manage their own emotions. Parents will be able to take full responsibility for their emotions, process them, and express them in healthy ways that benefit both the child's character formation and their relationship with their children." Whose side do you come down on, and why?

6. Discuss: "Should a father and mother treat their daughter's body the way they would want a future boyfriend or husband to treat her body?"

7. Agree, disagree, why: "The goal of parenting is never to break or crush a child's will. When parents release their child to the world as a late teen (even if they stay at home), their young adult children will benefit from a firm will so that they can act on their dreams."

8. Discuss: "I can connect the dots between a beating and the coerced obedience that endures for as long as the child fears the parent. I cannot connect the dots between the use of physical force against her body and the nurturing of problem solving skills valuable for decision-making and for managing impulses and emotions as she grows."

17

Joy

A Satisfyingly Creative Way of Life

1. The typical way we understand the emotion of joy is a "satisfyingly pleasant emotional response to favorable circumstances." But joy can be a core value. How are they different and how do they connect?

2. Agree, disagree, why: "Joy is hedonistic but not selfish. When joy explodes in our hearts, we want others in our heart. We spread the feeling."

3. I do not mention them in the chapter, but lots of writers and speakers disagree with the idea "Joy can be sought after." What do you think?

4. Do you think it hypocrisy to "rejoice with those who are rejoicing" when you don't feel like rejoicing or "relentlessly communicate thanks" when you do not feel thankful?

5. "It's wonderful when our joyful feelings lead our behavior; other times, our behavior has to step up and lead our emotions." What do you think?

6. How might "Work 3:1 into your daily routine" (Barbara L. Fredrickson) look in your life if you decided to live it?

7. What might a play ethic look like in your life?

8. What stands out for you from the discussion of the core value of creativity?

18

Love

Where There is No Sacrifice

1. How are "I love you" and "I'm in love with you" different? Why do I think "in love" is a bad reason for deciding on a marriage partner"? What do I offer in its place? What do you think?

2. Why do dating and engaged couples so often "ignore, postpone, and minimize problems"? What are the consequences?

3. What does "love loves the light" mean?

4. Agree, disagree, why: "When we have truth as a core value, we can come to a place where it is impossible to lie to the person we love, so deep is our love for that one person."

5. I think there is a place for selfishness in I love you. If you agree, where do you draw the line between healthy, appropriate selfishness and relationship-damaging selfishness?

6. What do you learn about I love you from Jesus' Parables of the Lost Sheep and the Lost Son (Luke 15)?

7. Discuss: "But to give your heart away in love, vulnerability, and without restraint to another person, to say I love you, is to open your heart to hungering for and needing that other person's love."

8. "There is no sacrifice in love." What do you think?

Bibliography

The Arbinger Institute. *Leadership and Self-Deception: Getting Out of the Box.* 2d ed. San Francisco: Berrett-Koehler, 2010.
Altidor, Welby. *Creative Courage: Leveraging Imagination, Collaboration, and Innovation to Create Success beyond Your Wildest Dreams.* Hoboken: Wiley, 2017.
Alvarez, Alfred. *The Savage God: A Study of Suicide.* London: Weidenfeld and Nicolson, 1971.
Axling, William. *Kagawa.* Rev. ed. New York: Harper, 1946.
Chin, Ba. *The Family.* Translated by S. Shapiro. 3d ed. Peking: Foreign Languages Press, 1978.
Bar-On, Reuven, and James D. A. Parker, eds. *Handbook of Emotional Intelligence: Theory, Development, Assessment, and Application at Home, School, and in the Workplace.* San Francisco: Jossey-Bass, 2000.
Ben-Shahar, Tal. *Happier: Learn the Secrets to Daily Joy and Lasting Fulfillment.* New York: McGraw Hill, 2007.
Ben-Ze'ev, Aaron. *The Subtlety of Emotions.* Cambridge: MIT Press, 2000.
Bennis, Warren, Daniel Goleman, and James O' Toole. *Transparency: How Leaders Create a Culture of Candor.* With Patricia Ward Biederman. San Francisco: Jossey-Bass, 2008.
Boyatzis, Richard, and Annie McKee. *Resonant Leadership: Renewing Yourself and Connecting with Others through Mindfulness, Hope, and Compassion.* Boston: Harvard Business School Press, 2005.
Bradshaw, John. *Healing the Shame That Binds You.* Rev. and enl. ed. Deerfield Beach: Health Communications, 2005.
———. *Post-Romantic Stress Disorder: What to Do When the Honeymoon is Over. New Discoveries about Lust, Love, and Saving Your Marriage Before It's Too Late.* Deerfield Beach: Health Communications, 2014.
Brooks, David. *The Road to Character.* New York: Random, 2015.
Brown, Brené. *Daring Greatly: How the Courage to be Vulnerable Transforms the Way We Live, Love, Parent, and Lead.* New York: Gotham, 2012.
———. *I Thought It Was Just Me (but it isn't): Telling the Truth about Perfectionism, Inadequacy, and Power.* New York: Gotham, 2007.
———. *The Gifts of Imperfection.* Center City: Hazeldon, 2010.
Buckingham, Marcus. *The One Thing You Need to Know: About Great Managing, Great Leading, and Sustained Individual Success.* New York: Free, 2005.
Cameron, Kim. *Positive Leadership: Strategies for Extraordinary Performance.* San Francisco: Berrett-Koehler, 2008.
Carnegie, Dale. *How to Win Friends and Influence People.* New York: Simon and Schuster, 1981.

Catmull, Ed. *Creativity, Inc. Overcoming the Unseen Forces that Stand in the Way of True Inspiration*. With Amy Wallace. New York: Random, 2014.

Chapman, Gary. *The 5 Love Languages: The Secret to Love that Lasts*. Chicago: Northfield, 1992.

———. *Things I Wish I'd Known Before We Got Married*. Chicago: Northfield, 2010.

Cloke, Kenneth, and Joan Goldsmith, *The Art of Waking People Up: Cultivating Awareness and Authenticity at Work*. Warren Bennis Signature Series. San Francisco: Jossey-Bass, 2003.

———. *Resolving Conflicts at Work: Ten Strategies for Everyone on the Job*. 3d ed. San Francisco: Jossey-Bass, 2011.

Collins, Jim. *Good to Great: Why Some Companies Make the Leap . . . and Others Don't*. New York: Collins Business, 2001.

———. *How the Mighty Fall: And Why Some Companies Never Give In*. New York: HarperCollins, 2009.

Collins, Jim, and Morten T. Hansen. *Great by Choice: Uncertainty, Chaos, and Luck — Why Some Thrive Despite Them All*. New York: HarperCollins, 2011.

Collins, Jim, and Jerry I. Porras. *Built to Last: Successful Habits of Visionary Companies*. New York: Collins, 2002.

Covitz, Joel. *Emotional Child Abuse: The Family Curse*. Boston: Sigo, 1986.

Crabb, Larry. *The Safest Place on Earth: Where People Connect and are Forever Changed*. Nashville: Word, 1999.

———. *Shattered Dreams: God's Unexpected Pathway to Joy*. Colorado Springs: Waterbrook, 2001.

Crafton, Barbara Cawthorne. *Jesus Wept: When Faith & Depression Meet*. San Francisco: Jossey-Bass, 2009.

Csikszentmihalyi, Mihaly. *Creativity: Flow and the Psychology of Discovery and Invention*. New York: HarperCollins, 1996.

———. *Flow: The Psychology of Optimal Experience*. New York: Harper and Row, 1990.

Dacey, John S., and Kathleen H. Lennon. *Understanding Creativity: The Interplay of Biological, Psychological, and Social Factors*. With Lisa B. Fiore. San Francisco: Jossey-Bass, 1998.

Damasio, Antonio. *Descartes' Error: Emotion, Reason, and the Human Brain*. New York: Penguin, 1994.

Danby, Herbert. *The Mishnah: Translated from the Hebrew with Introduction and Brief Explanatory Notes*. Oxford: Oxford University Press, 1933.

Davidson, Richard J. *The Emotional Life of Your Brain: How It's Unique Patterns Affect the Way You Think, Feel, and Live — and How You Can Change Them*. With Sharon Begley. New York: Hudson Street, 2012.

Duhigg, Charles. *The Power of Habit: Why We Do What We Do in Life and Business*. New York: Random, 2012.

Ekman, Paul. *Emotions Revealed: Recognizing Faces and Feelings to Improve Communication and Emotional Life*. 2d ed. New York: St Martin's Griffin, 2007.

Engel, Beverly. *Breaking the Cycle of Abuse: How to Move beyond Your Past to Create an Abuse-Free Future*. Hoboken: Wiley, 2005.

———. *The Emotionally Abused Woman: Overcoming Destructive Patterns and Reclaiming Yourself*. New York: Fawcett, 1990.

———. *The Emotionally Abusive Relationship: How to Stop Being Abused and How to Stop Abusing*. Hoboken: Wiley, 2002.

———. *Healing Your Emotional Self: A Powerful Program to Help You Raise Your Self-Esteem, Quiet Your Inner Critic, and Overcome Your Shame*. Hoboken: Wiley, 2006.

———. *Honor Your Anger: How Transforming Your Anger Style Can Change Your Life*. Hoboken: Wiley 2004.

———. *The Jekyll and Hyde Syndrome: What to Do if Someone in Your Life Has a Dual Personality — or If You Do*. Hoboken: Wiley, 2007.

———. *The Nice Girl Syndrome: Stop Being Manipulated and Abused — and Start Standing Up for Yourself*. Hoboken: Wiley, 2008.

———. *The Power of Apology: Healing Steps to Transform All Your Relationships*. New York: Wiley, 2001.

Erasmus of Rotterdam. *Praise of Folly and Letter to Martin Dorp 1515*. Translated by B. Radice. Penguin Classics. New York: Penguin, 1971.

Evans, Dylan. *Emotion: The Science of Sentiment*. Oxford: Oxford University Press, 2001.

Fiorina, Carly. *Tough Choices: A Memoir*. New York: Penguin, 2006.

Fossum, Merle A., and Marilyn J. Mason. *Facing Shame: Families in Recovery*. New York: Norton, 1986.

Foster, Richard J. *Money, Sex & Power: The Challenge of the Disciplined Life*. San Francisco: Harper and Row, 1985.

Fredrickson, Barbara L. *Love 2.0: How Our Supreme Emotion Affects Everything We Feel, Think, Do, and Become*. New York: Hudson Street, 2013.

———. *Positivity: Groundbreaking Research Reveals How to Embrace the Hidden Strength of Positive Emotions, Overcome Negativity, and Thrive*. New York: Crown, 2009.

Gardner, John W. *Self-Renewal: The Individual and the Innovative Society*. New York: Harper and Row, 1964.

Gay, Peter. *Freud: A Life for Our Time*. New York: Norton, 1988.

George, Bill. *Authentic Leadership: Rediscovering the Secrets to Creating Lasting Value*. Warren Bennis Signature Series. San Francisco: Jossey-Bass, 2003.

———. *7 Lessons for Leading in Crisis*. Warren Bennis Signature Series. San Francisco: Jossey-Bass, 2009.

———. *True North: Discover Your Authentic Leadership*. With Peter Sims. Warren Bennis Signature Series. San Francisco: Jossey-Bass, 2007.

Gergen, David. *Eyewitness to Power: The Essence of Leadership; Nixon to Clinton*. New York: Simon and Schuster, 2000.

Germer, Christopher K. *The Mindful Path to Self-Compassion: Freeing Yourself from Destructive Thoughts and Emotions*. New York: Guilford, 2009.

Gingrich, Heather Davediuk. *Restoring the Shattered Self: A Christian Counselor's Guide to Complex Trauma*. Downers Grove: InterVarsity, 2013.

Goleman, Daniel. *Destructive Emotions: How Can We Overcome Them? A Scientific Dialogue with the Dalai Lama*. New York: Bantam, 2003.

———. *Emotional Intelligence*. New York: Bantam, 1995.

———. *Focus: The Hidden Driver of Success*. New York: HarperCollins, 2013.

———. *The Meditative Mind: The Varieties of Meditative Experience*. New York: Putnam, 1988.

———. *Social Intelligence: The New Science of Human Relationships*. New York: Bantam, 2006.

———. *Vital Lies, Simple Truths: The Psychology of Self-Deception*. New York: Simon and Schuster, 1985.

———. *Working with Emotional Intelligence*. New York: Bantam, 1998.

Goleman, Daniel, and Warren Bennis. *The Power of Truth: A Leading with Emotional Intelligence Conversation*. Compact disc. New York: Audio Renaissance, 2006.

Goleman, Daniel, Richard Boyatzis, and Annie McKee. *Primal Leadership: Realizing the Power of Emotional Intelligence*. Boston: Harvard Business Review, 2002.

Goleman, Daniel, and Peter Senge. *Working with Presence: A Leading with Emotional Intelligence Conversation*. Compact disc. New York: Audio Renaissance, 2007.

Goleman, Daniel, Jack Welch, and Suzy Welch. *What Makes a Leader? A Leading with Emotional Intelligence Conversation*. Compact disc. New York: Audio Renaissance, 2006.

Grossman, Dave. *On Killing: The Psychological Cost of Learning to Kill in War and Society*. Rev. ed. New York: Back Bay, 2009.

Hall, Donald P. *Breaking Through Depression: A Biblical and Medical Approach to Emotional Wholeness*. Eugene: Harvest House, 2009.

Hart, Archibald D. *Adrenaline and Stress*. Nashville: Thomas Nelson, 1995.

———. *The Anxiety Cure: You Can Find Emotional Tranquility and Wholeness*. Nashville: Thomas Nelson, 1999.

———. *Unmasking Male Depression: Recognizing the Root Cause of Many Problem Behaviors, Such as Anger, Resentment, Abusiveness, Silence, Addictions, and Sexual Compulsiveness*. Nashville: Thomas Nelson, 2001.

Hawthorne, Nathaniel. *The Scarlet Letter*. 1850. New York: Knopf, 1992.

Herman, Judith Lewis. *Father-Daughter Incest*. Cambridge: Cambridge University Press, 1981.

———. *Trauma and Recovery*. New York: Basic, 1997.

Hume, David. *A Treatise on Human Nature*. 1738. Edited by L. A. Selby-Bigge. 2d ed. Oxford: Clarendon Press, 1978.

Hybels, Bill. *Axiom*. Grand Rapids: Zondervan, 2008.

———. *Courageous Leadership*. Grand Rapids: Zondervan, 2002.

———. "Vision to Die For." *The Global Leadership Summit 2007 Team Edition*. Barrington: Willow Creek Association, 2007. DVD.

Ibsen, Henrik. *The Wild Duck*. 1884. Drama Classics 75. Translated by S. Mulrine. London: Nick Hern, 2006.

Johnson, David, and Jeff van Vonderen. *The Subtle Power of Spiritual Abuse: Recognizing & Escaping Spiritual Manipulation and False Spiritual Authority within the Church*. Minneapolis: Bethany House, 1991.

Kagan, Jerome. *What is Emotion? History, Measures, and Meanings*. New Haven: Yale University Press, 2007.

Kaufman, Gershen. *Shame: The Power of Caring*. 2d ed. Rochester: Schenkman, 1985.

Kegan, Robert, and Lisa Laskow Lahey. *Immunity to Change: How to Overcome It and Unlock the Potential in Yourself and Your Organization*. Leadership for the Common Good. Boston: Harvard Business, 2009.

Kennedy-Moore, Eileen, and Jeanne C. Watson. *Expressing Emotion: Myths, Realities, and Therapeutic Strategies*. New York: Guildford, 1999.

King, Stephen. *On Writing: A Memoir of the Craft*. New York: Scribner, 2000.

Koestler, Arthur. *The Act of Creation*. London: Picador, 1969.

Kushner, Harold S. *The Book of Job: When Bad Things Happened to a Good Person.* New York: Schocken, 2012.

———. *Conquering Fear: Living Boldly in an Uncertain World.* New York: Knopf, 2009.

Lazarus, Richard S. *Emotion and Adaptation.* New York: Oxford University Press, 1991.

LeDoux, Joseph. *The Emotional Brain: The Mysterious Underpinnings of Emotional Life.* New York: Simon and Schuster, 1996.

Lencioni, Patrick. *The Five Dysfunctions of a Team: A Leadership Fable.* San Francisco: Jossey-Bass, 2002.

Lewis, C. S. *The Four Loves.* London: Geoffrey Bles, 1960.

———. *The Problem of Pain.* New York: Macmillan, 1944.

Lewis, Michael. *Shame: The Exposed Self.* New York: Free, 1992.

Lewis, Michael, Jeannette M. Haviland-Jones, and Lisa Feldman Barrett, eds. *Handbook of Emotions.* 3d ed. New York: Guildford, 2008.

Lewis, Michael, and Carolyn Saarni, eds. *Lying and Deception in Everyday Life.* New York: Guildford, 1993.

Longman III, Tremper. *Proverbs.* Baker Commentary on the Old Testament Wisdom and Psalms. Grand Rapids: Baker, 2006.

Luther, Martin. "On the Jews and their Lies." 1543. In *The Christian in Society,* 121–306. Edited by F. Sherman. Translated by M. H. Bertram. Vol. 47 of *Luther's Works: American Edition.* Philadelphia: Fortress, 1971.

Matthews, Gerald, Moshe Zeidner, and Richard D. Roberts. *Emotional Intelligence: Science & Myth.* Cambridge: MIT Press, 2002.

Maxwell, John C. *Developing the Leader within You.* Nashville: Thomas Nelson, 1993.

———. *Winning with People: Discover the People Principles That Work for You Every Time.* Nashville: Thomas Nelson, 2004.

McClelland, David C. *Human Motivation.* Cambridge: Cambridge University Press, 1987.

Melville, Herman. *Moby-Dick or The Whale.* 1851. New York: Penguin, 1988.

Miller, Alice. *Banished Knowledge: Facing Childhood Injuries.* Translated by A. Miller and L. Vennewitz. New York: Doubleday, 1990.

———. *The Body Never Lies: The Lingering Effects of Cruel Parenting.* Translated by A. Jenkins. New York: Norton, 2005.

———. *Breaking Down the Wall of Silence: The Liberating Experience of Facing Painful Truth.* Translated by S. Worrall. New York: Perseus, 2009.

———. *The Drama of the Gifted Child.* Translated by R. Ward. Rev. ed. New York: Basic, 1997.

———. *For Your Own Good: Hidden Cruelty in Child-Rearing and the Roots of Violence.* Translated by H. and H. Hannum. New York: Farrar, 2002.

———. *The Truth Will Set You Free: Overcoming Emotional Blindness and Finding Your True Adult self.* Translated by A. Jenkins. New York: Basic, 2001.

Moore, Thomas. *Original Self: Living with Paradox and Originality.* New York: HarperCollins, 2000.

Morrison, Toni. *Beloved.* New York: Knopf, 1987.

Nason-Clark, Nancy, and Catherine Clark Kroeger. *Refuge from Abuse: Healing and Hope for Abused Christian Women.* Downers Grove: InterVarsity, 2004.

Nathanson, Donald L., ed. *The Many Faces of Shame.* New York: Guildford, 1987.

Nay, W. Robert. *Taking Charge of Anger: Six Steps to Asserting Yourself without Losing Control.* 2d ed. New York: Guilford, 2012.

Neenan, Michael. *Developing Resilience: A Cognitive-Behavioural Approach.* New York: Routledge, 2009.
Neff, Kristin. *Self-Compassion: Stop Beating Yourself Up and Leave Insecurity Behind.* New York: HarperCollins, 2011.
Newsom, Carol A. *The Book of Job: A Contest of Moral Imaginations.* New York: Oxford University Press, 2003.
Nussbaum, Martha C. *The Therapy of Desire: Theory and Practice in Hellenistic Ethics.* Martin Classical Lectures. Princeton: Princeton University Press, 1994.
―――. *Upheavals of Thought: The Intelligence of Emotions.* Cambridge: Cambridge University Press, 2001.
Oatley, Keith. *Emotions: A Brief History.* Malden: Blackwell, 2004.
Palmer, Parker J. *A Hidden Wholeness: The Journey toward an Undivided Life; Welcoming the Soul and Weaving Community in a Wounded World.* San Francisco: Jossey-Bass, 2004.
―――. *Let Your Life Speak: Listening for the Voice of Vocation.* San Francisco: Jossey-Bass, 2000.
Pinker, Steven. *How the Mind Works.* New York: Norton, 2009.
Plath, Sylvia. *The Bell Jar.* London: Heinemann, 1963.
Plutchik, Robert. *Emotion: A Psychoevolutionary Synthesis.* New York: Harper and Row, 1980.
Popper, Karl R. *The Logic of Scientific Discovery.* London: Routledge, 1959.
―――. *The Open Society and Its Enemies.* 2 vols. 5th ed. Princeton: Princeton University Press, 1966.
Powell, Colin. *It Worked for Me: In Life and Leadership.* New York: HarperCollins, 2012.
Ridley, Matt. *Nature via Nurture: Genes, Experience, & What Makes Us Human.* New York: HarperCollins, 2003.
Rogers, Carl R. *On Becoming a Person: A Therapist's View of Psychotherapy.* Boston: Houghton Mifflin, 1961.
Ronson, Jon. *So You've Been Publicly Shamed.* New York: Penguin, 2015.
Rothschild, Babette. *The Body Remembers: The Psychophysiology of Trauma and Trauma Treatment.* New York: Norton, 2000.
Rubin, Theodore Isaac. *The Angry Book.* New York: Collier, 1969.
Sandborn, Calvin. *Becoming the Kind Father: A Son's Journey.* Gabriola Island: New Society, 2007.
Sawyer, R. Keith. *Explaining Creativity: The Science of Human Innovation.* Oxford: Oxford University Press, 2006.
Scazzero, Geri, and Peter Scazzero. *The Emotionally Healthy Woman: Eight Things You Have to Quit to Change Your Life.* Grand Rapids: Zondervan, 2013.
Scazzero, Peter. *Emotionally Healthy Spirituality: Unleash a Revolution in Your Life in Christ.* Nashville: Thomas Nelson, 2006.
Scazzero, Peter, and Warren Bird. *The Emotionally Healthy Church: A Strategy for Discipleship that Actually Changes Lives.* Grand Rapids: Zondervan, 2010.
Schiff, Stacy. *The Witches, Salem, 1692.* New York: Little, Brown, 2015.
Seinfeld, Jerry. *Seinlanguage.* New York: Bantam, 1993.
Sternberg, Robert J. Foreword to *Emotional Intelligence: Science & Myths,* by Gerald Matthews, Moshe Zeidner, and Richard D. Roberts, xi–xiii. Cambridge: MIT Press, 2002.

Scheff, Thomas J., and Suzanne M. Retzinger. *Emotions and Violence: Shame and Rage in Destructive Conflicts*. Lexington: Lexington, 1991.
Schneider, Carl D. *Shame, Exposure, and Privacy*. New York: Norton, 1977.
Seligman, Martin E. P. *Authentic Happiness: Using the New Positive Psychology to Realize Your Potential for Lasting Fulfillment*. New York: Free, 2002.
———. *Flourish: A Visionary New Understanding of Happiness and Well-Being*. New York: Free, 2011.
Senge, Peter C., Otto Scharmer, Joseph Jaworski, and Betty Sue Flowers. *Presence: Exploring Profound Change in People, Organizations, and Society*. New York: Random, 2004.
Shenk, Joshua Wolf. *Lincoln's Melancholy: How Depression Challenged a President and Fueled His Greatness*. Boston: Houghton Mifflin, 2005.
Smedes, Lewis B. *The Art of Forgiving: When You Need to Forgive and Don't Know How*. New York: Ballantine, 1996.
———. *Shame and Grace: Healing the Shame We Don't Deserve*. New York: HarperCollins, 1993.
Solomon, Andrew. *Far from the Tree: Parents, Children, and the Search for Identity*. New York: Scribner, 2012.
———. *The Noonday Demon: An Atlas of Depression*. New York: Scribner, 2001.
Tacitus. *Agricola, Germania, Dialogus*. Translated by M. Hutton and W. Peterson. Loeb Classical Library. Cambridge: Harvard University Press, 1970.
Tanakh: The Holy Scriptures; The New JPS Translation According to the Traditional Hebrew Text. Philadelphia: Jewish Publication Society, 1985.
Tharp, Twyla. *The Collaborative Habit: Life Lessons for Working Together*. With Jesse Kornbluth. New York: Simon and Schuster, 2009.
———. *The Creative Habit: Learn It and Use It for Life*. With Mark Reiter. New York: Simon and Schuster, 2006.
Twenge, Jean M., and W. Keith Campbell. *The Narcissism Epidemic: Living in an Age of Entitlement*. New York: Free, 2009.
Van der Kolk, Bessel A. *The Body Keeps the Score: Brain, Mind, and Body in the Healing of Trauma*. New York: Viking, 2014.
Voltaire. *Candide*. Translated by L. Bair. New York: Bantam, 1959.
Welch, Jack. *Winning*. With Suzy Welch. New York: HarperCollins, 2005.
White, Jr., Ronald C. *A. Lincoln: A Biography*. New York: Random, 2009.
Wiesel, Elie. *Night*. Translated by S. Rodway. New York: Bantam, 1960.